A Gift for

_____

Presented by

_____

I Used to
Know That
LITERATURE

I Used to Know That

LITERATURE

Inside Stories of Famous Authors,
Classic Characters, Unforgettable
Phrases, and Unanticipated Endings

C. ALAN JOYCE & SARAH JANSSEN

Reader's
Digest

The Reader's Digest Association, Inc.
New York, NY / Montreal

A READER'S DIGEST BOOK

FOR READER'S DIGEST
U.S. Project Editor: Kim Casey
Copy Editor: Ellen Bingham
Editorial Assistance: Rachael Handler, Lauren Hanson
Indexer: Lina Burton
Project Designer: Elizabeth Tunnicliffe
Senior Art Director: George McKeon
Illustrator: Olga Shevchenko
Manufacturing Manager: Elizabeth Dinda
Associate Publisher: Rosanne McManus
President and Publisher, Trade Publishing: Harold Clarke
Editor-in-Chief, Reader's Digest North America: Liz Vaccariello

ISBN 978-1-60652-415-2

Previously published as *Under the Covers and Between the Sheets*.

The Library of Congress has cataloged the original edition as follows:
        Joyce, C. Alan.
Under the covers and between the sheets : the inside story behind classic characters,
authors, unforgettable phrases, and unexpected endings /
C. Alan Joyce & Sarah Janssen.
        p. cm.

 ISBN 978-1-60652-034-5

1. Literature--Miscellanea. 2. Literary curiosa. I. Janssen, Sarah, 1982- II. Title.
PN43.J69 2009
802--dc22

                                        2009020644

We are committed to both the quality of our products and the service
we provide to our customers. We value your comments, so please feel
free to contact us.

                The Reader's Digest Association, Inc.
                Adult Trade Publishing
                44 South Broadway
                White Plains, NY 10601

For more Reader's Digest products and information, visit our website:
                www.rd.com (in the United States)
                www.readersdigest.ca (in Canada)

Printed in the United States

1 3 5 7 9 10 8 6 4 2

"Do you realize that all great literature—*Moby Dick, Huckleberry Finn, A Farewell to Arms, The Scarlet Letter, The Red Badge of Courage, The Iliad* and *The Odyssey, Crime and Punishment*, the Bible, and "The Charge of the Light Brigade"—are all about what a bummer it is to be a human being?"

—Kurt Vonnegut

CONTENTS

OFF THE PAGE 138

Unbelievable facts about familiar characters
(and the writers who created them)

One for the Books

Admit it: Even though you're a ravenous reader today, you probably still wince and shudder when someone mentions *The Scarlet Letter,* and you are overcome by memories of that high school English teacher who slowly squeezed the life out of what *technically* should have been a fun read for a 16-year-old. Seriously: It's got sin, adultery, revenge, self-flagellation, mysterious astronomical portents…what's not to like?

Or maybe you break out in a cold sweat when you see a copy of *Moby Dick.* (How many allegories can you pack into one book, anyway?)

Or your eyes glaze over every time you recall the end of James Joyce's "The Dead." (How the heck do you hear snow "falling faintly through the universe"?)

Or you start feeling queasy when you spot a copy of Upton Sinclair's *The Jungle.* (We get it; meat-packing plants were super-disgusting.)

We've all been there. No matter how much you love literature, there's probably a roomful of authors and a mountain of books you would go out of your way to avoid reading again. But just because you studied the dickens out of Dickens in high school, that doesn't mean you know the whole story—or even the most intriguing parts if it.

Wouldn't *David Copperfield* have seemed a tiny bit more interesting if you knew the author had a strange fascination with human corpses (page 31)? Would you have enjoyed *On the Road* a little more if you knew that Kerouac's original manuscript ended, in effect, with a note that "the dog ate my homework" (page 37)? And wouldn't it have been mildly reassuring to know that even the gentlemanly Mark Twain, upon opening *Pride and Prejudice*, was overcome with the urge to dig up Jane Austen and "beat her over the skull with her own shin-bone" (page 125)?

On the other hand, maybe you adore every last scrap of "serious" literature—but you think science fiction is second-class writing and the exclusive province of pocket-protector–wearing men. If so, you probably didn't know that 2007 Nobel Prize winner Doris Lessing has been churning out fantastic sci-fi for years... or you've overlooked the works of Octavia Butler, the first science fiction writer to win a MacArthur "Genius" Grant (page 55).

Think that the James Bond novels are a far-fetched waste of time? Take a closer look: Some of Ian Fleming's real-life WWII experiences (he was a British intelligence officer, after all) directly inspired Bond's daring exploits (page 65). And all those preposterously sexy romance novels? They're kid stuff, compared to the steamy personal lives of their authors, complete with broken homes, illegitimate children, and seductive handymen (pages 68–71). We will admit that not every book has a silver lining, so to speak, but even the dreariest prose can provide a few laughs—so toward that end, we've rounded up the worst of the worst writing of all time, both intentional and embarrassingly unintentional (pages 78–81).

Speaking of kid stuff, we've also unearthed little-known facts about classic children's authors—from the Brothers Grimm to J. K. Rowling—that cast their lives and books in a whole new light. We've got the scoop on the real endings of classic fairy tales (hint: Cinderella had less kissing, more eye-gouging pigeons); the long, strange trip that turned Fifi the monkey into Curious George (page 88); and some decidedly child-unfriendly works by beloved authors like Shel Silverstein, who penned a pop song about venereal disease (page 93).

Or maybe you read any fiction you can get your hands on, while nonfiction always feels like homework? There's a reason that the phrase "stranger than fiction" is cliché—sometimes the true story is infinitely more interesting than the imagined tale. Remember the scandal over author James Frey, who duped Oprah Winfrey into endorsing his "memoir"? He wasn't the first (or the last) author to deceive the talk-show doyenne (page 107). And you never know what you'll find inside someone's diary...especially if it belonged to Albert Einstein's last girlfriend, who documented his relatively curious treatment for avian depression (page 123).

And when you've grown tired of all the curious facts that lie under the covers, there's even more to be found off the page entirely—from the revered poet who once worked as a "prostitute manager" to pay the bills (page 146), to the less-than-successful investment strategies of Mark Twain (page 152), to a 1940s precursor to TV's *Big Brother*, where a gaggle of oversexed authors and artists (and one legendary stripper) set up house together in Brooklyn (pages 158–59).

There's much more to be found between the sheets that follow, including publishers' rejection letters for now-classic works of fiction; the original vampire craze, 200 years before *Twilight*; a concise guide to the greatest chain-smoking, pistol-packing private dicks in crime fiction; the most offensive books you've ever loved; and the secret rock & roll lifestyle of some of the biggest best-selling authors of all time. We hope you'll enjoy discovering these secrets as much as we did.

Shot Out of the Canon

Most of the authors and works profiled here stand among "serious" literature's all-time greats, but don't let that scare you away. We've rounded up all the stories your English Lit teacher didn't tell you about—the authors who almost succeeded in destroying their greatest works, addictions that fueled the creation of classic novels, and some of the downright *weirdest* books ever written. Want to seem like an instant literary expert (without really trying)? It's all right here.

THE GREATEST BOOKS NEVER WRITTEN

In the words of poet John Greenleaf Whittier: "For of all sad words of tongue or pen, / The saddest are these: 'It might have been!'" These writers left behind unfinished writing that—had they lived to see it through—might have surpassed even their greatest published works.

A REAL COOL DROOD

Charles Dickens serialized many of his works in popular magazines, ending each installment with a cliff-hanger ending that left readers wanting more. It's a great system ... unless the author dies in the middle of the project, as Dickens did while writing *The Mystery of Edwin Drood*. At the time of his death in 1870, Dickens had completed only 6 out of 12 planned installments and left few notes or clues about his plans for the rest of the story. The question "Who killed Edwin Drood?" has engaged Dickens scholars and fans practically since the day of his death. In 1914 members of the Dickens Fellowship, a group that included G. K. Chesterton and George Bernard Shaw, staged a mock trial of John Jasper, the character most often believed to be the murderer (Shaw, as foreman of the jury, said that the evidence was scant but that Jasper should be found guilty of manslaughter ... if only to spare the jury from the possibility of being murdered in their sleep). At least four films and dozens of theatrical versions have run the story out to various conclusions, and a 1985 Broadway musical gave audience members the chance to vote on the identity of the murderer. And Drood-mania shows no sign of subsiding: As recently as 2009, two new novels (Dan Simmons's *Drood* and Matthew Pearl's *The Last*

Dickens) used the unfinished manuscript as a jumping-off point for murder mysteries of their own.

A GREATER GATSBY?

F. Scott Fitzgerald's *The Great Gatsby* (1925) is routinely held up as one of the greatest works of American fiction. His three other complete novels (*This Side of Paradise*, 1920; *The Beautiful and the Damned*, 1922; and *Tender Is the Night*, 1934) are held in high regard, but generally pale in comparison to Fitzgerald's great Jazz Age portrait. Had he completed his final novel, *The Last Tycoon* (1941), many believe it could have surpassed even *Gatsby*: According to a *New York Times* review from 1941, "...uncompleted though it is, one would be blind indeed not to see that it would have been Fitzgerald's best novel and a very fine one." The chapter Fitzgerald was working on, on the day before he died, brought it roughly halfway to completion, at 60,000 words; it has been rumored that Fitzgerald asked his friend Nathaniel West (author of *Day of the Locust*) to help him finish it if he died before he could complete the task...but tragically, West and his wife were killed in a car crash one day after Fitzgerald's death. (The book was re-released in 1994 under Fitzgerald's original title, *The Love of the Last Tycoon*.)

PHILIP MARLOWE AND THE MARITAL MYSTERY

When mystery master Raymond Chandler died in 1959, he left behind one of the toughest unsolved cases of his career: How in the world would legendary gumshoe Philip Marlowe cope with marriage to *The Long Goodbye*'s femme fatale, Linda Loring? Chandler completed only four first-draft chapters (about 40 typed pages) of the book that would ultimately become *Poodle Springs*

Mystery (1989) with a little help from detective novelist Robert Parker, creator of the Spenser series. Chandler himself offered little help in solving the case, noting in a 1958 letter: "I don't know whether the marriage will last or whether [Marlowe] will walk out of it or get bounced."

....

"I finished the thing; but I think I sprained my soul."

—KATHERINE ANNE PORTER, ON HER NOVEL *SHIP OF FOOLS*

....

THE HAND THAT FEEDS YOU

After ingratiating himself to the leading lights of New York City high society for decades, *Breakfast at Tiffany's* scribe, Truman Capote, took a startling turn with his final, unfinished book, *Answered Prayers:* He turned his sharp eye (and pen) back toward the glamorous jet-setters who had shared all their secrets with the diminutive, oddly mannered writer. Capote hyped the unseen book for years, promising it would be his "Remembrance of Things Past," and finally bowed to public pressure by publishing three chapters in *Esquire* in 1975 and 1976. The response from his so-called friends was swift and harsh: According to legendary New York gossip columnist Liz Smith, "Never have you heard such gnashing of teeth, such cries for revenge, such shouts of betrayal and screams of outrage." In response, Capote defended his actions: "I'm a writer, and I use everything. Did all those people think I was there just to entertain them?" The rest of the manuscript has never surfaced—to the relief of scores of New York "ladies who lunch," no doubt—though Capote claimed the complete novel was finished and stored in a safe-deposit box...whose key has yet to be found.

NOTHING IS CERTAIN BUT DEATH AND TAXES

David Foster Wallace showed few signs of scaling back his infamously verbose style in his follow-up to the heady, footnote-laden *Infinite Jest* (1996). Within a year of its publication, Wallace had begun working on a manuscript about IRS employees and the nature of boredom, for which he dove into a deep study of accounting and tax procedures. Wallace had expressed a desire to make his next work more accessible, but as the text ran up to several hundred thousand words, Wallace began calling the new book simply "The Long Thing." In 2008 after years of struggling with depression, he organized his computer files, neatly stacked the unfinished manuscript for his wife, and hung himself; the unfinished manuscript was to be published in 2010, under the title *The Pale King*.

> *"This book is an agglomeration of lean-tos and annexes and there is no knowing how big the next addition will be, or where it will be put. At any point, I can call the book finished or unfinished."*
>
> **—ALEXANDER SOLZHENITSYN, IN *THE OAK AND THE CALF***

WASTE NOT, WANT NOT

As the adage goes, "If you want something done, you've got to do it yourself." For whatever reason, some famous authors requested that their papers and manuscripts be destroyed upon their death; lucky for us, their literary executors weren't always so good at following orders.

AN INCOMPLETE HISTORY

Virgil, the preeminent poet of the Roman Empire, is said to have written the *Aeneid* at the request of Caesar Augustus, who wanted a chronicle of Rome's greatness under his rule. Virgil died with the work still incomplete in 19 B.C. and had instructed his literary executor, Varius, to destroy the existing text. Fortunately for us (and, we suppose, Augustus), Varius didn't comply, and Virgil's 11 years of work on the *Aeneid* still stands as one of the great works of classical literature.

Augustus's request may have been influenced somewhat by Virgil's *Eclogues:* In the fourth pastoral poem, Virgil prophesied that a child, presumed to be Augustus (maybe only by Augustus?), had been born to bring a golden age of peace, order, and prosperity. For what it's worth, readers of the same poem in the Middle Ages interpreted it as a prophesy of the birth of Jesus.

A TRILOGY IN ONE PART

Somewhat lesser known to American readers than Russian contemporaries like Tolstoy and Dostoyevsky, writer Nicolai Gogol nonetheless exerted a huge influence on the development of the novel—Dostoyevsky once remarked that every Russian realist to follow actually emerged "from under Gogol's greatcoat."

Unfortunately, we have no idea just how great (or overrated) more of his work might have been. Gogol was attempting to expand his novel *Dead Souls* into a trilogy in line with Dante's *Divine Comedy*, but he inexplicably destroyed the nearly completed second part, then died nine days later.

WITH FRIENDS LIKE THIS...

Emily Dickinson was an enormously productive poet, writing nearly 1,800 poems before her death in 1882. Of course, no one knew that until after she died: She published fewer than a dozen poems in her lifetime. Dickinson's work would have been lost forever had her sister Lavinia not half-broken her promise to Emily. A prolific letter writer, Emily had made Lavinia promise to burn all her papers following her death. But when Lavinia discovered the trove of poems that no one knew existed, she refused to burn the verses. She did destroy Emily's letters, so perhaps Dickinson only half turned over in her grave.

BETTER OFF DEAD

Most people wouldn't look kindly on a person who disobeyed their friend's dying wish—but would most likely make an exception for Max Brod, who saved Kafka from the incinerator. Much of Kafka's work wasn't published until Brod championed it after Kafka's death, completely disregarding a stipulation in Kafka's will that his work be burned. Though Brod was ultimately overshadowed by his friend's posthumous successes, he had been a much more successful writer than Kafka was in his lifetime and ended up editing or appending much of the work Kafka left behind.

The Castle, for instance, stopped in midsentence, and *Amerika,* Kafka's story about a visitor in a country he would never himself have visited, was originally titled "The Man Who Disappeared" (the phrase was resurrected as a subtitle for some editions).

HIS BETTER HALF

Even when Vladimir Nabokov was alive, his wife, Vera, had to stop him from destroying his manuscripts: She once ran out of the house and snatched pages of what would become *Lolita* from a backyard bonfire. But a dying Nabokov made it clear that he wanted his final, fragmentary manuscript—consisting of about 50 handwritten index cards—destroyed after his death, which occurred in 1977. Instead, Vera placed them into a Swiss safe-deposit box for safekeeping while she decided what to do. Upon her death more than a decade later, responsibility for the decision—destroy or preserve? publish or not publish?—fell to Dmitri Nabokov, the couple's son. After seesawing over the decision for years, Nabokov announced in 2008 that he would publish *The Original of Laura;* he claimed that his father appeared to him in a dream and announced, "You're stuck in a right old mess—just go ahead and publish!" We'll believe it when we see it.

....

"Paper is cheap, and authors need not now erase one book before they write another."

—HENRY DAVID THOREAU

....

WRITING UNDER THE INFLUENCE

It's no secret that many writers have had substance abuse issues—some have practically made whole careers of it. Alcoholism, drug abuse, and writing don't always go hand in hand, but for these writers addiction was equal parts inspiration and albatross.

....

"An alcoholic is someone you don't like, who drinks as much as you do."

—DYLAN THOMAS

....

GENTLY INTO THAT GOOD NIGHT

The Welsh poet Dylan Thomas (1914–53) spent many of the final days of his alcohol-soaked life traveling in the United States on college reading tours. As he became more widely known, the tours also afforded Thomas opportunities to hobnob (and drink) with celebrities. On one besotted occasion, Thomas was seen urinating on a plant in Charlie Chaplin's house. Of course, Thomas's career as a poet and a drinker ended tragically early. One night, at the age of 39, the story goes, he bragged about consuming 18 whiskeys, calling it a record, then fainted and died in the hospital several days later. In actuality, Thomas died of pneumonia—and despite his affinity for whiskey, an autopsy showed his liver to be remarkably clear of cirrhosis.

LAUDABLE LAUDANUM?

Just a few of the writers who enjoyed this common opium-based drug in the 19th century included Charles Dickens, Elizabeth Barrett Browning, and Sir Walter Scott. Allusions to Barrett Browning's habit can be found in the infamous Barrett Browning love poems, in the form of red poppies.

AT WIT'S END

After her stinging one-liners, acerbic critic and writer Dorothy Parker (1893–1967) may be best known for three-martini lunches with the Algonquin Round Table in the 1920s. Along with alcoholism, however, came the complications; Parker attempted suicide several times before dying of natural causes. With no children or other close relatives, she left her entire estate to Martin Luther King Jr., who would be assassinated the next year.

> *"I hate to advocate drugs, alcohol, violence, or insanity to anyone, but they've always worked for me."*
>
> —HUNTER S. THOMPSON

UNSAFE AT ANY SPEED

Jean-Paul Sartre's (1905–80) longtime companion, Simone de Beauvoir, catalogued his use of amphetamines (up to 200 mg per day) and sleeping pills, which he often washed down with whiskey (presumably to take the edge off all those amphetamines). Sartre began work on *Saint Genet* (1952) as a 50-page introduction to a book collecting Jean Genet's writings, but, overstimulated, the work grew to 800 pages.

Science fiction author Philip K. Dick (1928–82) was also a heavy user of amphetamines and countless other drugs, both recreationally and because he believed they enhanced his productivity. He eventually suffered permanent pancreatic damage because of his many Schedule I pursuits, but he may not have been as prolific without them. In one year (1963–64), he produced 11 novels and innumerable essays, short stories, and plot treatments.

SPEED BUMP

W. H. Auden, who took amphetamines daily for 20 years beginning in 1938, called the pills a "labor-saving device" in the "mental kitchen"—"very crude, liable to injure the cook, and constantly breaking down."

FEAR AND LOATHING AND WILD TURKEY

From Chivas-drinking and Dunhill chain-smoking, to varying levels of abuse of just about every psychedelic or psychotropic controlled substance, Hunter S. Thompson's (1937–2005) drug use was as much a part of his writing as was his politics (though he once managed to share a limo with Richard Nixon, on the condition that they talk only about football). His drug use could sometimes be a detriment to his productivity: In one cocaine-fueled episode, Thompson, in Africa to cover the 1974 "Rumble in the Jungle" between Muhammad Ali and George Foreman, gave away his tickets so he could go for a swim in the hotel pool.

....

> *"There is no such thing as bad whiskey. Some*
> *whiskeys just happen to be better than others.*
> *But a man shouldn't fool with booze until he's fifty;*
> *then he's a damn fool if he doesn't."*
>
> —**William Faulkner**

....

DRINKS OF A DIRTY OLD MAN

Charles Bukowski (1920–94) began drinking at the age of 13 as a defense mechanism against an abusive father. In his novels, alter ego Henry (Hank) Chinaski binges in barrooms in reflection of Bukowski's own liver-abusing days and nights, whether while working for the postal service—as Bukowski did for 12 years—or gambling at the horse track (a favorite Bukowski hobby). Bukowski finally left his odd jobs behind when John Martin, publisher of Black Sparrow Press, promised his life savings, in $100-a-month increments for life, if Bukowski would write full time. The money was enough to keep him in rent, smokes, and booze—though Bukowski eventually made a little money from the actual sale of his writing, too.

WILLIAM TELL

Drunk and possibly high at a Mexico City party in 1951, William Burroughs (1914–97) suggested to Joan Vollmer—the mother of his son—that they do their "William Tell" act. Burroughs accidentally shot Vollmer in the process, killing her. Burroughs said many times that he never would have become a writer if not for the incident. In *Queer*, which he began writing while awaiting his trial, he wrote, "So the death of Joan brought me in contact with the invader, the Ugly Spirit, and maneuvered me into a lifelong struggle, in which I have had no choice except to write my way out." (He was given a two-year suspended sentence.)

MISERY

Acclaimed horror writer Stephen King (1947–) struggled with addiction to drugs and alcohol frequently during his writing career—to the point where he doesn't remember finishing or revising some of his best-known books, including *It* (1986). His wife, Tabitha, held an intervention in 1987, pouring out the contents of his trash can in front of friends and family, including "cocaine in gram bottles and cocaine in plastic Baggies, coke spoons caked with snot and blood, Valium, Xanax . . ." King stayed off drugs for many years, until he became addicted to Oxycontin after he was hit by a van in 1999. "I had to kick it the way a junkie kicks heroin . . . I didn't sleep for two weeks. My feet twitched uncontrollably—that is why it is called kicking the habit; your feet literally kick out. It was horrible."

THE ORIGINAL "COFFEE ACHIEVER"

Compared to some of the addictions of his fellow literary legends, Honore de Balzac's (1799–1850) principal addiction—to coffee!—seems downright tame. Who hasn't relied on a few extra cups to get through an all-night study session or to polish off a particularly irksome piece of prose? But Balzac took it much, much further: He practically couldn't breathe without the stuff. The corpulent writer is said to have downed 50 cups a day of thick Turkish coffee…and when he couldn't wait for the next cup to brew, he would chomp on a handful of raw beans to keep the buzz alive. Mainlining caffeine helped him maintain an incredibly prolific output, but it also drove him to an early grave: Balzac succumbed to a constellation of ailments, including high blood pressure, at age 51.

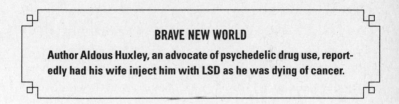

BRAVE NEW WORLD

Author Aldous Huxley, an advocate of psychedelic drug use, reportedly had his wife inject him with LSD as he was dying of cancer.

UNDER THE INFLUENCE

British poet Samuel Taylor Coleridge (1772–1834) was known to disappear on opium binges for days at a time, during which he could produce astonishing work: He said that the images of his great poem *Kubla Khan* came to him in a vivid opium dream. But not all of his efforts under the influence were so successful…or at least, so scholars used to think. In 1814 Coleridge was commissioned to translate Goethe's poem *Faust* into English, but he never delivered a completed manuscript and presumably spent the advance to feed his growing addiction. But in 2007 a new translation of *Faust* emerged, purportedly written by Coleridge; according to Professor James McKusick, who studied the text since the 1970's, Coleridge did complete the translation, but for *another* publisher—and probably insisted that it be published anonymously (in 1821) to prevent the original publisher from coming after him to recoup its advance.

THE METHODS OF THEIR MADNESS

The writing tools, rituals, and obsessions that fueled the world's best-known authors, from nudity and rented typewriters to ... visits to the morgue?

UNDER A "SENTENCE" OF DEATH

In 1959 Anthony Burgess received some life-changing news: Doctors told him that he had an inoperable brain tumor and that he had one year left to live. Driven by a need to provide for his wife after his supposedly inevitable demise, Burgess wrote five novels in an incredible rush over the next year ... and then published *A Clockwork Orange* in 1962 ... and kept on churning out novels until 1993 (outliving his wife in the process), when he finally succumbed to *lung* cancer, with more than 30 novels to his name.

THE ORIGINAL "DIME NOVEL"?

In the late 1940s, Ray Bradbury became fascinated with the history of book burning in different civilizations. Gradually, the seed of an idea began to form about firemen who burned books, but with a vocal newborn daughter at home, Bradbury had trouble focusing on the text. He didn't have enough money to rent an office, but one day, while wandering around the UCLA campus, he found a basement room full of typewriters that could be rented for 10 cents per half hour. He promptly rounded up a bag of dimes and holed up in that room for nine days, tapping out a novella called *The Fireman* that he later expanded into *Fahrenheit 451*. Total cost for writing the story? $9.80.

THEY TOOK IT LYING DOWN

Though Marcel Proust, Mark Twain, and Truman Capote were all ambitious and prolific writers, you wouldn't necessarily have known it from observing them at work: Each was famously fond of lying down on the job. Proust's housekeeper noted that she "never saw him write even the shortest note standing up...He didn't even prop himself up on the pillow." Twain rebuked authors who complained about the difficulty of writing, saying "Writing is the easiest thing in the world...Just try it in bed sometime. I sit up with a pipe in my mouth and a board on my knees, and I scribble away." And Capote claimed, "I can't think unless I'm lying down"— especially with a cigarette and coffee. One imagines that Capote must have gone through a lot of cigarettes and coffee in bed, since his strict writing ritual also required him to produce two full drafts in longhand before he ever approached a typewriter (where revisions had to be typed on "a very special kind of yellow paper").

STAND UP AND BE COUNTED

Many authors—including Ernest Hemingway, who reportedly wrote *A Moveable Feast* at a stand-up desk—went the opposite route, preferring to do most of their writing on their feet. Philip Roth has said that he stands and paces almost continuously while working and that each page of his books probably represents about one-half mile of walking (which makes his National Book Award–winning first book, *Goodbye, Columbus,* roughly equal to a 100-mile trek). Charles Dickens also wrote on his feet and found inspiration by putting one in front of the other...but while strolling, he sometimes heeded a very peculiar call: "Whenever I am in Paris," he once said, "I am dragged by invisible force into the Morgue." Ah, Paris!

LITERATURE "BUFFS"

The bloggers of today didn't invent the practice of writing in their pajamas (or even less): Some of the greatest writers in history were known to write *au naturale.* Playwright Edmond Rostand (*Cyrano de Bergerac*) cooled his heels in the bathtub while working; D. H. Lawrence found inspiration by climbing trees in the nude (a kink that, to the best of our knowledge, never found its way into his books); and on at least one occasion, Victor Hugo is said to have conquered writer's block by giving a servant his clothes, locking himself in his room, and making the servant promise not to return until Hugo had finished his day's writing.

THE LIGHT AT THE END OF THE TUNNEL

Unlike many authors who let the narrative flow where it may, John Irving always likes to know where he's going. He has claimed that whenever he starts a new book, he tries "to write the last sentence first, even the last several paragraphs."

DO HIS PARTICIPLES DANGLE, TOO?

Leave it to best-selling author Dan Brown to think outside the box, even when it comes to his writing habits: When he hit a block trying to write anagrams for the book *Angels & Demons,* he got the creative juices flowing by hanging upside-down in gravity boots— a habit he carried through his work on *The Da Vinci Code,* along with frequent breaks for push-ups, sit-ups, and stretching.

THE BLIND READING THE BLIND

Legend has been built around Beethoven composing after he lost his hearing completely—but, likewise, many classic texts were written by authors who couldn't read the words on their pages.

- It *would* figure that the so-called "Blind Bard" probably wasn't vision-impaired in the slightest, wouldn't it? Homer—the author of the preliterate epics *The Odyssey* and *The Iliad*—didn't exactly leave a written record of his life, so Homer's reputation as a blind, itinerant poet may have developed as a figment of history's collective imagination. The theories on why history put Homer down as blind range from the literal (in some dialects, variations on the word "homer'"were defined as "one who does not see") to the presumed (*The Odyssey* features a blind man telling stories about Troy—it doesn't take a huge leap to wonder if that character was self-referential).

- Argentine writer Jorge Luis Borges began his career as a librarian but was "promoted" to the post of poultry inspector as a presumed punishment for his criticism of Juan Peron's authoritarian regime (he didn't take the job). When Peron was removed from office, Borges was appointed director of Argentina's National Library—but he had already lost his sight. Borges called the circumstances proof of "God's splendid irony, in granting me at once 800,000 books and darkness."

- John Milton "sacrificed his sight, and then he remembered his first desire, that of being a poet," according to Borges. After focusing for years on his philosophical tracts, the newly blind Milton returned to his attempts at the masterpiece epic *Paradise Lost.* He did all his "writing"—that is, composing—at night; the next day, he dictated the mentally honed verses.

- *All the King's Men* author and poet-laureate Robert Penn Warren had been preparing to enter the Naval Academy at age 16, but his brother forced a change of plans when he threw a stone that blinded Warren in one eye. Warren instead attended college at Vanderbilt University, and there he attempted suicide when he mistakenly began thinking that he was also losing sight in the other eye as a result of "sympathy syndrome."

- Pulitzer Prize–winner Alice Walker also lost an eye to sibling hijinks: Walker and two brothers were playing a game of cowboys and Indians using all-too-real B.B. guns as weapons, and Walker was struck in the eye. Like Warren, Walker feared for decades losing her sight completely, which she attributed to a doctor casually telling her as a five-year-old, "Eyes are sympathetic . . . the other will likely become blind, too."

- James Joyce was essentially blind by the time he began work on *Finnegan's Wake,* so he relied on a pool of friends and aspiring writers to take dictation. One of these assistants was a young Samuel Beckett; during one of their sessions, Joyce heard a knock at the door and said "Come in," which Beckett dutifully wrote down. Upon hearing the text read back to him, Joyce questioned the odd phrase . . . but then decided to "let it stand" in the final manuscript, yet another curious puzzle for scholars to decode.

YES, BUT IS IT ART?

You thought *Moby Dick* was tough reading? Try these on for size: These are works of serious literature, where some are written without verbs, without punctuation ... or even without the letter "e."

James Joyce, *Finnegan's Wake* (1939): Joyce said that this opaque and multilayered text was meant "to keep the critics busy for three hundred years" (so check back with us in 2239, when all its secrets will presumably have been uncovered). The text draws inspiration from the historical theories of Italian philosopher Giambattista Vico; forms a closed narrative loop, with the first sentence of the book completing the final sentence; and makes liberal use of invented words, derived from dozens of languages. Among these are a collection of hundred-letter words representing "thunderclaps," which announce the start of each age of history. (Example: Bababadalgharaghtakamminarronnkon nbronntonnerronntuonnthunntrovarrhounawnskawntoo-hoohoordenenthurnuk.) What could be simpler?

Ernest Vincent Wright, *Gadsby: Champion of Youth* (1939): Though many writers had written shorter works under similar conditions, Wright challenged himself to write a complete novel without using the letter "e": The 50,110-word *Gadsby* is the staggering result. The preface notes that as he wrote, "a whole army of little E's gathered around my desk, all eagerly expecting to be called upon." Years later, Georges Perec accepted the same challenge, producing *La Disparition* (A Void) in 1969. The French original and English translation also omitted the letter "e"—but the Spanish translation omitted "a," the most common letter in that language, instead.

Jerzy Andrzejewski, *Bramy Raju* (*Gates of Paradise*) (1961): Andrzejewski's serious novella about the Children's Crusade of 1212 clocks in at 40,000 words...but only one sentence, with no punctuation except commas.

Vladimir Nabokov, *Pale Fire* (1962): The ostensible "text" of Nabokov's peculiar book is a 1,000-line narrative poem (entitled "Pale Fire") by the fictional poet John Shade—but the real story is told through accompanying commentary and footnotes that overwhelm the poem and comprise the bulk of the book.

William Gaddis, *JR* (1975): Twenty years after publication of his über-challenging *The Recognitions*, Gaddis returned with this story about an 11-year-old who creates a business empire from a pay phone in his school—told in more than 700 pages of nearly pure dialogue, creating a symphony (or cacophony, depending on your attention span) of interweaving voices and conversations.

Michel Thaler, *Le Train de Nulle Part* (*The Train from Nowhere*) (2004): Thaler's 233-page novel offers plot, character, action...but not a single verb. According to Thaler, "The verb is like a weed in a field of flowers. You have to get rid of it to allow the flowers to grow and flourish. Take away the verbs and the language speaks for itself." In June 2004, the author (whose real name is Michel Dansel) even held a ceremony to "bury" the verb at Paris's Sorbonne University.

Mark Z. Danielewski, *House of Leaves* (2000): This bizarre book—which seems to be equal parts horror novel, film analysis, memoir, and collage—is about a house with more space inside than outside, hiding an unseen and presumably evil force. One of the book's multiple narratives analyzes a film about the house, another analyzes that analysis...and in the meantime, text flows in all directions on the page, interspersed with meandering footnotes and eye-straining layout tricks.

Hannu Luntiala, *Viimeiset Viestit* (*The Last Message*) (2007): If a novel like this was going to be written, it was inevitably going to come from Finland, the home of Nokia: Luntiala's book is written entirely in text messages—about 1,000 of them, covering more than 300 pages. We just hope that the main characters had bargain-basement rates on their cell-phone service.

DOGGONE IT

The original manuscript for *On the Road* was written on a 119-foot-long scroll of paper. Literature lovers have long been able to visit the scroll at exhibitions in museums and libraries across the country. However, no one knows exactly how long the manuscript was when Kerouac completed it or what the treatise's original ending lines were. Kerouac's handwriting appears at the end of the scroll, noting that a cocker spaniel belonging to Lucien Carr, a friend (and the father of writer Caleb Carr), had eaten the last lines.

YOU DON'T SAY?

Many commonly used words, phrases, and proverbs were coined or popularized in classic works of fiction, though they didn't always mean what we think they do today. Find out more than you ever cared to know about the ones you've used (and possibly abused) for years.

TOO MUCH OF A GOOD THING

So many common expressions (including the title of this section) originated in Shakespeare's work that it would be impossible to name them all. Here are a few of the more familiar turns of phrase for which the Bard deserves credit:

All's well that ends well	*All's Well That Ends Well* (1602)
All the world's a stage	*As You Like It* (1600)
Fair play/foul play	*The Tempest* (1610–11), among others
Give the devil his due	*Henry IV, Part I* (c. 1597)
Green-eyed monster	*Othello* (1603)
Love is blind	*The Merchant of Venice* (1597)
Neither a borrower nor a lender be	*Hamlet* (1603)
Rhyme nor reason	*Comedy of Errors* (1590)
Send him packing	*Henry IV, Part I* (c. 1597)
There's a method in my madness (literally, "Though this be madness yet there is method in it.")	*Hamlet* (1603)
The long and short of it	*The Merry Wives of Windsor* (c. 1597)
We have seen better days	*Timon of Athens* (1607)
Wear your heart on your sleeve	*Othello* (1603)
Wild-goose chase	*Romeo and Juliet* (1592)

ISN'T IT IRONIC?

"Sweets to the sweet" isn't exactly the corny-yet-well-intentioned expression it appears to be, so you might want to pick a different phrase for your next candygram. Spoken by Hamlet's mother over Ophelia's grave, the phrase actually refers to the "sweet"-smelling funeral flowers she brought to cover the "sweet" smell of a decaying body.

AUTHOR! AUTHOR!

There are countless words based on author's names, but most of those words simply add an adjectival suffix to the author's name and are used to describe something that relates to the style of the writer referenced (Shakespearean stands as a good example). A handful, however, are elevated to meanings beyond "in the style of":

Bowdlerize: He couldn't have been the only one to find Shakespeare's bawdier bits offensive, but Thomas Bowdler—a writer and editor—is the only one who did something about it, sparing prudish readers everywhere. His 10-volume *Family Shakespeare* (1818) cut out anything that might disturb the sensibilities of readers—creating a collection that was reprinted many times. He also thought enough of himself to edit and publish censored versions of the Old Testament (1822) and Gibbon's *History of the Decline and Fall of the Roman Empire* (1826). So Bowdler is justly honored with an original eponym of his very own—*bowdlerize* now refers to any instance of removing or censoring indelicate references or vocabulary from a text.

Orwellian: Thank goodness George Orwell had the presence (or prescience?) of mind to write *1984* and *Animal Farm,* or we wouldn't have a quick term to describe grim, totalitarian dystopias. Fortunately, whenever something reminds us of a threat to a free society—especially if some form of misinformation, propaganda, or truth denial is involved— we can describe it thusly. Especially if there's some sort of ominous Big Brother–style overseer involved (another term we can thank Orwell for).

Kafkaesque: Much like Kafka's work itself, the meaning of Kafkaesque is somewhat amorphous, but one good catch-all definition is Merriam-Webster's: "Having a nightmarishly complex, bizarre, or illogical quality." The disorienting feeling this definition implies would, of course, be quite familiar to Gregor Samsa.

CLEARING THROUGH THE RED TAPE

A fact of modern life, bureaucratic red tape was once tangible rather than metaphorical—lawyers and government officials in England bound documents together with actual red tape made of cloth or ribbon. Charles Dickens was the first writer to use the term metaphorically in *Bleak House* (1852–53): "[We] think to keep away the Wolves of Crime and Filth by our...gentlemanly handling of red tape."

WHAT A CHARACTER!

Some characters are just so memorable that their names become synonymous with their most outstanding personality traits. Of course, sometimes that means the new word describes a trait that has less-than-flattering associations. (How many girls have you met named Lolita?)

What the Dickens? We can only guess what Charles Dickens had in mind when he named the miserly focal character Ebenezer Scrooge in *A Christmas Carol* (1843)—especially given the fact that there is no evidence that Scrooge was an established English surname. But what do we care? It comes in handy now and then in describing the cheapskates and misanthropes among us—and not just during the holiday season.

"They Misunderestimated Me" Centuries before President George W. Bush became the admitted modern master of misspeaking, Richard Sheridan's *The Rivals* (1775) coined the word malapropism with the character Mrs. Malaprop. Of course, there was already a Latin word for these bumbling turns of phrase (*acyrologia,* for what it's worth), but Mrs. Malaprop made it her own by sheer virtue of opening her mouth, describing one person as "the very *pineapple* of politeness." Hopefully, fans of the play, in Mrs. Malaprop's own words, "might *reprehend* the true meaning of what she is saying."

Elementary, My Dear Eponym It may be most commonly used as sarcasm against the not-so-observant, but Sherlock Holmes's first name is still listed in dictionaries today as a synonym for detective. So ease up on your unperceptive friends (they may just take you seriously, anyway).

Sunny-Side Up The more cynical probably shudder at the notion of playing the "Glad Game," invented by Eleanor Porter's titular *Pollyanna* (1913). But at least when someone tells them to turn those lemons into lemonade, they have a better word for describing the irrepressibly optimistic, in several parts of speech—Pollyanna, Pollyannaism, and Pollyannaish are technically all words. And for those who revel in appreciating a glass half full, there's always Littleton, New Hampshire's, Official Pollyanna Glad Day, an annual June festival.

It Isn't Nice to Call Names He probably didn't set out to expand the list of synonyms for a sexually precocious young girl, but Vladimir Nabokov's memorable title character in *Lolita* (1955) and his character Humbert Humbert's own term nymphet are listed in Merriam-Webster's dictionary with that definition.

DOUBLE BIND

Catch-22 is one of those terms that is more often misused than not. As described in Joseph Heller's 1961 novel of the same name, Catch-22 is a rule or set of circumstances that inherently denies a solution to a problem, usually by employing circular logic. It appears most notably as the rule that keeps mentally ill WWII pilots from grounding themselves: "Orr would be crazy to fly more missions and sane if he didn't, but if he was sane he had to fly them. If he flew them he was crazy and didn't have to; but if he didn't want to he was sane and had to."

MAKE IT WORK

'Generation X'—from Douglas Coupland's 1991 novel *Generation X: Tales of an Accelerated Culture*—originally referred to those born in the late 1950s and 1960s. Though those identified today as members of Generation X are a few years younger than the characters Coupland described, certain generic characteristics are the same. One of Coupland's Gen-Xers admits to working a "McJob"—a term that Coupland didn't coin but is credited with forcing into the popular vernacular. A McJob was defined by Coupland as "a low-pay, low-prestige, low-dignity, low-benefit, no-future job in the service sector." Needless to say, the term is a nod to a popular fast-food franchise that shall remain nameless: The company threatened to sue when McJob was added to Merriam-Webster's dictionary and has formally campaigned to have it redefined to reflect "a job that is stimulating, rewarding... and offers skills that last a lifetime."

SCIENCE NONFICTION

Sci-fi giant Isaac Asimov is too often credited with inventing the word robot, which was actually coined by Czech playwright Karel Capek in *R.U.R.* (*Rossum's Universal Robots,* 1920). Technically, you could argue that Asimov gets a half credit on this one, though, because he was the first to use the term robotics in reference to the science of robots, in 1941—and Asimov *does* deserve full credit for his three laws of robotics.

Many other scientific concepts were originally named in fictional works:

Zero gravity/zero-G: Jack Binder first described zero gravity as a concept in 1938, though he wasn't referring to outer space: Binder was describing the center of the Earth's core.

Sci-fi savant Arthur C. Clarke coined zero-G in *Islands in the Sky* (1952), when his protagonist had to adapt to the physical effects when visiting a space station in Earth's orbit.

EAT IT AND WEEP

You can thank Robert Burns for giving us the most commonly sung holiday song (after "Happy Birthday," of course) when you're warbling to "Auld Lang Syne" on New Year's Eve. But unless you live in Scotland, you're probably missing out on Burns Night—for some, an equally boozy tradition. Across Scotland the week of January 25, highly structured "Burns suppers" honor the birth of the 18th century bard, complete with a recitation of Burns's poem "Address to a Haggis," which toasts the much-maligned main course for the evening. (Haggis, the unofficial national dish of Scotland, is a sheep's stomach stuffed with a mixture of sheep organs, oatmeal, onion, and other spices.) And, of course, Burns Night also concludes with a singing of "Auld Lang Syne."

Deep space: E. E. Smith is credited with using the term first in 1936, to refer to space far removed from one's home planet, in his seminal *Lensman* series. Outside of science fiction, its definition has changed since then to refer to something far more local—most scientists use the term to refer to space outside the Earth's atmosphere.

Pressure suit: Worn to maintain consistent pressure levels in space, the pressure suit was another product of E. E. Smith's imagination. Fortunately for Buzz Aldrin and his pals at NASA, their suits didn't follow Smith's sartorial design exactly—sparing us the sight of U.S. astronauts floating in fur-covered space suits.

THE DARK SIDE

David Gerrold was the first to call a self-replicating computer program a "virus" in 1972, in *When HARLIE Was Won,* which was nominated for Hugo and Nebula awards in 1972. But he's probably more famous for another self-replicating creation: Gerrold wrote the infamous *Star Trek* episode "The Trouble with Tribbles."

Ion drive: Imagined and named by Jack Williamson in *The Equalizer* (1947), more than a few spacecraft since have been powered in the same way—propulsion created by charged-particle emission.

THE OTHER FINAL FRONTIER

The term *cyberspace* first appeared in William Gibson's short story "Burning Chrome" (1982), and much of Gibson's seminal *Neuromancer* (1984) takes place in that same virtual plane of data, or "consensual hallucination experienced daily by billions of legitimate operators." Gibson said later that cyberspace—combining the words "cybernetics" and "space"—was conceived of as a buzzword—"evocative and essentially meaningless" with "no real semantic meaning."

"Individual science fiction stories may seem as trivial as ever to the blinder critics and philosophers of today— but the core of science fiction, its essence . . . has become crucial to our salvation if we are to be saved at all."

—ISAAC ASIMOV

EVERYONE'S A CRITIC

Some writers were famously friendly and supportive of each other's work—Herman Melville even dedicated *Moby-Dick* to his friend Nathaniel Hawthorne "in token of my admiration for his genius." But it's equally likely that they hate other writers' work (or just despise the writers themselves). In fact, it's probable that no one critiques writers as cruelly as their own kind. Here are a few of the more revered, on the writers they despised the most:

- "I cannot stand Tolstoy, and reading him was the most boring literary duty I ever had to perform, his philosophy and his sense of life are not merely mistaken, but evil, and yet, from a purely literary viewpoint, on his own terms, I have to evaluate him as a good writer." —AYN RAND

- "Poor Faulkner. Does he really think big emotions come from big words? He thinks I don't know the ten-dollar words. I know them all right. But there are older and simpler and better words, and those are the ones I use." —ERNEST HEMINGWAY, having been informed that William Faulkner believed that Hemingway "had no courage" and "had never been known to use a word that might send the reader to the dictionary."

- "That's not writing, that's typing." —TRUMAN CAPOTE on Jack Kerouac's *On the Road*

- "This is not at all bad, except as prose," —GORE VIDAL on Herman Wouk's *The Winds of War*

- "At certain points, reading the work can even be said to resemble the act of making love to a three-hundred-pound woman. Once she gets on top, it's over. Fall in love, or be asphyxiated." —**NORMAN MAILER**, on Tom Wolfe's *A Man in Full*

- "No more than the greatest mind ever to stay in prep school." —**NORMAN MAILER**, on J. D. Salinger

- "Every word she writes is a lie, including 'and' and 'the'." —**MARY MCCARTHY** on Lillian Hellman

- "The characters are nearly indistinguishable. A man in a wheelchair cannot just be a man in a wheelchair; he must be a vehicle to help a lame metaphor get around. Such is the method of the Well-Crafted Short Story." —**COLSON WHITEHEAD** on Richard Ford's short-story collection *A Multitude of Sins* (Two years later, Ford responded by spitting on Whitehead.)

CAN'T NOT PUT IT DOWN?

You can stop feeling guilty for giving up halfway through George Eliot's *Middlemarch* or Marcel Proust's *In Search of Lost Time* (nee *Remembrance of Things Past*). Turns out many fancy-pants authors do the same thing. Canadian short-story doyenne Alice Munro admitted as much in a 2001 interview with *The Atlantic,* noting that she was rereading Dostoyevsky's *The Brothers Karamazov*— not necessarily because she enjoyed it so much, but because she missed so much the first time around, when she skipped "the parts about money."

JUST SAY NO

Even the most-lauded writers have received a rejection letter or two from publishers or agents before they were awarded their Pulitzers and Nobels, but thankfully many persist. The excerpts below—including text from rejection letters, as well as publishers' "reader's reports" on submitted manuscripts—might have any aspiring writer rethinking his vocation.

James Baldwin
(1924–87)

Giovanni's Room (1956) was called "hopelessly bad."

Jorge Luis Borges
(1899–1986)

Submissions said to be "utterly untranslatable."

Pearl Buck
(1892–1973)

Pulitzer Prize–winning *The Good Earth* (1931) was rejected because Americans are "not interested in anything on China."

William Faulkner
(1897–1962)

Of *Sanctuary* (1931), which Faulkner claimed to have "deliberately conceived to make money," his editor said, "Good God, I can't publish this. We'd both be in jail."

Anne Frank
(1929–45)

The reader found Frank's diary to be "a dreary record of typical family bickering, petty annoyances, and adolescent emotions," commenting that it wouldn't sell due to a lack of familiar or appealing characters. "Even if the work had come to light five years ago, when the subject was timely," the reader wrote, "I don't see that there would have been a chance for it."

Tony Hillerman
(1925–2008)

Hillerman was told by an agent to "get rid of all that Indian stuff."

Jack Kerouac
(1922–69)

"His frenetic and scrambling prose perfectly express the feverish travels of the Beat Generation. But is that enough? I don't think so."

John le Carré
(1931–)

A publisher sent his submission to a colleague with a note: "You're welcome to le Carré—he hasn't got any future."

Ursula K. Le Guin (1929–)

The Left Hand of Darkness (1969) was "endlessly complicated by details of reference and information, the interim legends become so much of a nuisance despite their relevance, that the very action of the story seems to be to become hopelessly bogged down and the book, eventually, unreadable."

Vladimir Nabokov (1899–1977)

Lolita (1955) was considered "...overwhelmingly nauseating, even to an enlightened Freudian... the whole thing is an unsure cross between hideous reality and improbable fantasy. It often becomes a wild neurotic daydream...I recommend that it be buried under a stone for a thousand years."

Anaïs Nin (1903–77)

"There is no commercial advantage in acquiring her, and, in my opinion, no artistic."

George Orwell (1903–50)

Animal Farm (1945) was declined because it is "impossible to sell animal stories in the U.S.A."

Sylvia Plath (1932–63)

"There certainly isn't enough genuine talent for us to take notice."

Marcel Proust (1871–1922)

One editor said in response to the tome *In Search of Lost Time*, also known as *Remembrance of Things Past* (published in English, 1922–31), "My dear fellow, I may be dead from the neck up, but rack my brains as I may I can't see why a chap should need 30 pages to describe how he turns over in bed before going to sleep."

HORTON HEARS A "NO!"

Dr. Seuss's (1904–91) *And to Think That I Saw It on Mulberry Street...* **(1937) was rejected by publishers 27 times before Vanguard Press agreed to publish it. His subsequent success as a children's author didn't make him immune to rejections, though. Random House rejected Seuss's proposal for a book on how to write for children in 1949, saying, "Some of them would feel an author-artist of picture books could hardly qualify as an expert in the field of juvenile writing."**

GUILTY PLEASURES

Airport books, whodunits, page-turners, bodice rippers, potboilers, best sellers.... There are many names for so-called genre fiction, but that last one is the most important. And even though you'll find some bad books in any of these genres, you'll find there are a lot of "classics" on these shelves as well, from Jane Austen to H. G. Wells. So here's to dusting off that Georgette Heyer or reading your Tom Clancy in public again— there is no shame in that.

THE ROOTS OF PULP FICTION

In the early years of the 20th century, pulp fiction came into its own. Given this moniker because pulp's stories and serialized novels were printed in magazines on cheap pulpwood paper, pulp fiction created or evolved many of the genre fictions as we know them today. Pulp fiction was the ultimate in populist literature, priced at less than half the cost of weightier magazines. It introduced American readers to writers as diverse as Edgar Rice Burroughs, Raymond Chandler, Dashiell Hammett, H. P. Lovecraft, and Tennessee Williams, in monthly pulps. Initial general-interest pulps like *Argosy* (established in 1896), and *All-Story* (1905) eventually ceded the market to specialized titles like *Black Mask* (detective stories from 1927 on), *Weird Tales* (1923), and *Western Trails* (1938).

....

> *"I have been a soreheaded occupant of a file drawer*
> *labeled 'Science Fiction'... and I would like out,*
> *particularly since so many serious critics regularly*
> *mistake the drawer for a urinal."*

—KURT VONNEGUT (1922–2007)

....

SCIENCE FICTION, SCIENCE FACT

These science-fiction writers didn't just write about spaceships and little green men: Some were eerily prescient about future technology, while others left a mark on pop culture that extended well beyond the printed page. And a surprising number of women writers proved that they could "geek out" as well as any man.

THE FUTURE IS NOW

Sir Arthur C. Clarke (1917–2008) is perhaps best known as the author of the novel *2001: A Space Odyssey*. Unlike most book-to-film adaptations, the novel was written during the production of the film, in close collaboration with director Stanley Kubrick, and published after the movie was released. If you've seen only the film, you may be surprised to learn that the alien monoliths of Kubrick's film have something in common with Dorothy's ruby slippers in *The Wizard of Oz*. Those slippers were gleaming silver in L. Frank Baum's book, but they were changed to ruby red in the movie version to better showcase Technicolor film stock. Similarly, the monoliths in Clarke's book were translucent crystal but became solid black in Kubrick's film.

If alien monoliths are ever found on the Moon, the safer bet is that they would be translucent crystal; Clarke is celebrated for making accurate predictions of various technologies years ahead of their time. In 1945 he predicted that geostationary satellites would make ideal relays for television and other communication signals—and to this day, the geostationary orbit (22,369 miles [36,000 km] above the Earth) is known as a "Clarke Orbit."

Clarke is in good company: A surprising number of modern-day inventions and technologies were predicted decades ahead of their time by science-fiction writers.

AUTHOR PREDICTED	BECAME REALITY IN
Jules Verne (1828–1905) Lunar travel, in *From the Earth to the Moon* (1865)	**1969:** *Apollo 11* crew walks on the moon
Edward Bellamy (1850–1898) Credit cards, in his novel *Looking Backward* (1888)	**1950:** First modern credit card (Diner's Club) is introduced
H. G. Wells (1866–1946) Automatic sliding doors, in the story *When the Sleeper Wakes* (1899)	**1954:** Invented by Dee Horton and Lew Hewitt; triggered by stepping on a mat
Hugo Gernsback (1884–1967) Individualized news reports, in *Ralph 124C 41+* (1925)	**2002:** Google News goes live in September
Aldous Huxley (1894–1963) Test-tube babies, in *Brave New World* (1932)	**1978:** Louise Joy Brown, the first test-tube baby, is born in England
Ray Bradbury (1920–) Full-wall, flat-screen TVs, in *Fahrenheit 451* (1953)	**1971:** First LCD panels shown to the public; as of 2009, LCD and plasma screens more than 100 inches (254 cm) across are available
Douglas Adams (1952–2001) Electronic books, in the form of the eponymous *Hitchhiker's Guide to the Galaxy* (1979)	**1990s:** Early handheld e-book readers on sale; first Amazon Kindle, with built-in wireless connection, available in 1997

THE FIRST LADY
OF SCIENCE FICTION

Though its many movie adaptations and derivatives have fallen more within the horror genre, Shelley's *Frankenstein* (originally subtitled "The Modern Prometheus") is more accurately viewed as science fiction—and one of the earliest examples of the genre, made all the more notable for being written by a teenage girl. The genesis of the book is almost as weird as the story itself. On a rainy evening in 1816 at the poet Lord Byron's villa in Geneva, a group of guests (including Mary and her husband, Percy Shelley) participated in a challenge to see who could write the best ghost story. Byron gave up after a few pages, and Percy wrote a fragment of verse . . . but Mary took the challenge seriously. Within a few days, she had begun the text of *Frankenstein*, partly inspired by recent scientific experiments performed by Erasmus Darwin (Charles's grandfather).

MAN ON THE MOON

Jules Verne (1828–1905) predicted lunar travel with particularly uncanny accuracy in *From the Earth to the Moon* (1865). In Verne's book and in reality, the United States launched the first manned spacecraft (with a three-man crew) to land on the moon. The craft was launched from Florida and splashed down in the Pacific Ocean. His spacecraft was even similar in size to *Apollo 11*: 8,730 kg for Verne's *Columbiad* versus 11,920 kg for *Apollo 11*. But Verne's capsule had the advantage in creature comforts: On the return flight, Verne's astronauts unwound with a bottle of fine wine.

IT'S A MAN'S WORLD BUT A WOMAN'S UNIVERSE

**Think sci-fi is mainly a playground for nerdy boys
(and the men they grow into)? Think again.
These women rank among the giants of the genre:**

Author	Recommended Reading	Noteworthy Facts
Gertrude Barrows Bennett	*The Citadel of Fear* (1918)	Published under the name "Francis Stevens"; one of H. P. Lovecraft's major influences
Andre Norton (Alice Mary Norton)	*Witch World* (1963)	Named a Grand Master of the Science Fiction Writers of America
James Tiptree Jr. (Alice Bradley Sheldon)	"Love Is the Plan the Plan Is Death" (1973)	Award is given in her (Tiptree's) name each year for a new sci-fi work that best explores gender issues
Doris Lessing	*Shikasta* (1979)	Winner of the 2007 Nobel Prize in Literature
Joan Vinge	*The Snow Queen* (1980)	Robert Heinlein dedicated his novel *Friday* (1982) to Vinge, Le Guin, and other notable women in sci-fi
Octavia Butler	*Bloodchild* (1995)	First sci-fi writer to win a MacArthur Genius Grant
Ursula K. Le Guin	*The Dispossessed* (1974)	Received Library of Congress Living Legend award

GROUND CONTROL TO MAJOR JON

Literary wunderkind Jonathan Lethem made his reputation with *Motherless Brooklyn* and *Fortress of Solitude,* but his first four published novels (*Gun, with Occasional Music*; *Amnesia Moon*; *As She Climbed Across the Table*; *Girl in Landscape*) were all well within the conventions of traditional sci-fi. Anyone who knew the teenage Lethem could have seen this coming: He cites his earliest "novel" as a 125-page unpublished work entitled *Heroes* (named for the David Bowie song), which he wrote over summer vacation at age 15.

REACHING FOR THE STARS

Sci-fi writers have too many surprises up their sleeves to limit themselves to one medium. In some cases, they wrote their really fantastic (and cinematic) stories specifically to be told on-screen, instead of on a page.

Theodore Sturgeon: Sturgeon was Kurt Vonnegut's inspiration for the character Kilgore Trout (see pages 114 and 139–40) and was a prolific sci-fi writer. Though his written work didn't reach a very wide audience, he did pen scripts for several curious episodes of the original *Star Trek* television series. In "Amok Time," the stoic Dr. Spock is afflicted with "Pon Farr," a hormonal condition that will kill him unless he returns to his home planet to mate; the episode also introduced the Vulcan salute, "Live long and prosper." In "Shore Leave," the *Enterprise* crew confronts an assortment of bizarre characters on the surface of an unexplored planet—including a samurai, a medieval knight, and characters from *Alice in Wonderland*. And in a third, unproduced episode, Sturgeon introduced one of the central tenets of the *Star Trek* universe: the Prime Directive, which dictates non-interference with alien cultures encountered by Federation ships.

Harlan Ellison: Ellison ranks as one of classic sci-fi's elder statesmen, with scores of stories and essays to his name; he also ranks as perhaps its most litigious representative. In 2009 he sued Paramount Home Entertainment for licensing revenue based on his award-winning script for the *Star Trek* episode, "The City on the Edge of Forever." Said the colorful Ellison in his own press release: "Am I doing this for other writers, for Mom (still dead), and apple pie? Hell no! I'm doing it for the 35-year-long disrespect and the money!"

William Gibson: Cyberpunk originator William Gibson (see page 45) and fellow author Tom Maddox wrote two episodes of *The X-Files*—dealing, naturally, with artificial intelligence, computers, and other common Gibsonian themes—as well as an early version of the movie *Alien 3*. But even Gibson's sci-fi cred couldn't save that script, which did away with series star Ripley (Sigourney Weaver) and turned the famously face-hugging aliens into an ebola-like airborne virus.

SPEAK GEEK?

GTW/CS/L/MD d-- s:+ a? C++++$ UL++++$ UC++$ US+++$
P++++$ L+++$ E--- W+++$ N+++ o+ K+++ !w--- O- M+ V-
PS+++ PE Y++ PGP+ !t 5? X-- !R(+++) tv-- b+++ DI++++/++ !D
G+ e+++ h++/-/--- r++ z?

That's how über-brainy sci-fi writer Charles Stross describes
himself in "geek code" on his website. The code, created by Robert
Hayden in 1993, translates various personal attributes into brief
codes. For example, Stross's code identifies him as a geek of tech-
nical writing, computer science, literature, and medicine (GTW/
CS/L/MD), who is of average height and above-average round-
ness (s:+), has no interest in *The X-Files* (X--), and reads several
books a week (b+++).

....

"When people talk about genre, I guess they men-
tion my name first, but without Richard Matheson,
I wouldn't be around. He is as much my father as
Bessie Smith was Elvis Presley's mother."

—STEPHEN KING

....

SCARE TACTICS

Who doesn't love a good scare? From vampire legends to the zombie apocalypse (it's coming, we swear!), these authors are guaranteed to send a shiver through your reading list.

NOT IF YOU WERE THE LAST MAN ON EARTH

According to the poet Robert Frost, "Some say the world will end in fire, some say in ice." How (and when) has it ended in other writers' apocalyptic works?

BOOK	THE END OF THE WORLD
Mary Shelley, *The Last Man* (1826)	**2090–2100:** Plague of natural origin decimates England (and presumably, the human race)
Richard Matheson, *I Am Legend* (1954)	**1976–79:** Bacterial plague transforms humans into bloodthirsty vampires
Stephen King, *The Stand* (1978)*	**1980:** Plague of man-made origin decimates the human race
Paul Auster, *In the Country of Last Things* (1987)	**Year unknown:** Cause unknown
Tim LaHaye & Jerry B. Jenkins, *Left Behind* (1995)	**Any day now:** Rapture, tribulation, second coming of Christ
Cormac McCarthy, *The Road* (2006)	**Year unknown:** Unspecified disaster covers planet with ash and destroys all plant and animal life

* King revised the second edition to take place in 1990. At the time of this publication, he doesn't seem to have received more recent information about the end of the world.

BLOODY GOOD FUN

If you thought the frenzy over Stephenie Meyer's *Twilight* series was intense, you must not have lived through the vampire crazes of the 18th and 19th centuries (and thus—phew—you're probably not a vampire yourself!). In the early 1700s, a fascination with blood-sucking monsters was fueled by reports of people exhuming corpses in Eastern Europe and "killing" them again, after those people supposedly rose from the grave and killed others in their region.

The word vampire officially entered the English language in 1734, according to the *Oxford English Dictionary,* though the vampires of the time weren't quite what we imagine today. Fear of crosses and holy water were common to many early vampire stories, as was the ability to transform into animals or mist. But not all vampires had pointy teeth: Many sucked blood through their victims' skin or suffocated them in their sleep. The vampires' lack of a shadow or reflection was mostly limited to German legends, while Romanian versions added sensitivity to garlic as a characteristic.

Most 18th-century vampire literature was in verse (even Goethe penned a poem about the undead), but in the 19th century it came into its own as one of the great types of horror fiction. Here are some notable bloodsuckers from that era, up to and including the greatest of them all:

John Polidori's *The Vampyre* (1819) was technically born on the same night in 1816 as Shelley's *Frankenstein* (see page 54). When Byron abandoned his horror-story idea, Polidori (Byron's personal physician) picked it up and produced the first vampire novel in English. Polidori reportedly couldn't stand Byron and made the title character a thinly veiled portrait of the great poet as a bloodthirsty ghoul. Ironically, Polidori's publishers attributed early printings of the novel to Byron to increase sales.

James Malcolm Rymer's *Varney the Vampire* **(1845–47)** was a popular "penny dreadful" (a cheap, illustrated work of fiction published as a series of slim pamphlets) that had a strong influence on later vampire fiction. Rymer had a curious fascination with blood-letting protagonists: He was also the author of the best-known penny dreadful, *Sweeney Todd.*

Carmilla **(1872),** by the Irish ghost-story writer Joseph Sheridan le Fanu (nicknamed "The Invisible Prince" for his reclusive nature and nocturnal writing habit), is viewed by some as the first lesbian vampire novel. Echoes of the book can be found in Stoker's work, notably in Count Dracula's vampiric female attendants, and in the fact that the vampire's bite didn't automatically turn victims into vampires themselves.

Bram Stoker's *Dracula* **(1897)** wasn't the first, but is certainly the most influential vampire novel of all time. Stoker drew inspiration from 18th-century legends, earlier vampire verse and novels...and his boss, Sir Henry Irving, a famous actor and manager of London's Lyceum Theatre. Stoker idolized Irving and served as his personal assistant and business

BAD DECISION

While traveling in America, Stoker and Irving met Mark Twain and agreed to invest in one of Twain's many doomed mechanical enterprises (see page 152). When the business began to sour, an embarrassed Twain wrote to Stoker, asking him to tell Irving that "when the wreckage floats ashore, he will get a good deal of his $500 back; and a dab at a time, I will make up to him the rest."

manager for 27 years, and many of the Count's mannerisms and physical characteristics are said to be based on his flamboyant employer. Some modern scholars have even claimed that Stoker harbored a repressed love for Irving; an allegedly heartbroken Stoker suffered a stroke a few weeks after Irving died in 1905, though he continued to write, with some impairment, until his death in 1912.

FAMOUS FIRST WORDS

"It is a truth universally acknowledged that a single man in possession of a good fortune, must be in want of a wife."

—Jane Austen, *Pride and Prejudice* (1813)

"It is a truth universally acknowledged that a zombie in possession of brains must be in want of more brains."

—Seth Grahame-Smith,
Pride and Prejudice and Zombies (2009)

THE WRITING DEAD

Much as the early 1700s were marked by a vampire craze, so too may the first years of the 21st century be remembered as a kind of "zombie renaissance" in the literary world, with a surprising flood of titles about the brain-devouring undead—some of them even appropriate for timid types who couldn't stomach *Night of the Living Dead*. For readers who want to check "zombie apocalypse" off their disaster-preparedness list, there's *The Zombie Survival Guide* (2003) by "preeminent zombie expert" Max Brooks, which covers such essential knowledge as the relative merits of rifles and flamethrowers when defending against zombie hordes. Or for the classically minded (and anyone who ever wished there were more zombie romance novels), there's Seth Grahame-Smith's *Pride and Prejudice and Zombies* (2009), which mashes up liberal chunks of Austen's original text with plenty of "ultraviolent zombie mayhem," and adds "martial arts master" to the list of qualities that draw Mr. Darcy to heroine Elizabeth Bennet. We imagine this is one Austen book that Mark Twain may have enjoyed (see page 125).

KUBRICK AND KING'S "SHADOW" WRITER

Love it or loathe it, Stanley Kubrick's adaptation of King's *The Shining* ranks as one of the most memorable horror films of all time. But for his big stab (pun intended) at making a scary movie, Kubrick almost adapted Diane Johnson's novel *The Shadow Knows*. Although he chose to film King's novel, Kubrick was dissatisfied with King's own screenplay; instead, Kubrick enlisted Johnson as his co-screenwriter for the film. Their script ultimately diverged from King's text in significant ways—to King's great disappointment—most notably with the addition of the now-iconic hedge maze scene.

....

"There's a lot to like about it. But it's a great big beautiful Cadillac with no motor inside. You can sit in it, and you can enjoy the smell of the leather upholstery—the only thing you can't do is drive it anywhere."

—STEPHEN KING, ON STANLEY KUBRICK'S
ADAPTATION OF *THE SHINING*

....

THE THRILL OF A LIFETIME

Action! Intrigue! Suspense! Some readers just can't resist a rollicking good thriller, and these authors have mastered the genre. From the courtroom to the operating room, here are (Shocking! Heart-pounding!) facts about some of the greatest suspense novelists around.

THE PEN IS MIGHTIER THAN THE SCALPEL

Best-selling thriller novelist Tess Gerritsen dreamed of writing Nancy Drew books as a child, but she ended up becoming a doctor. When a patient gave her a sack of romance novels, Gerritsen was bitten by the writing bug again and ended up writing her own romantic suspense thriller while on maternity leave. She later shifted to medical thrillers—including the rather un-Nancy-Drew-like *Harvest*, which featured Russian criminals stealing organs from orphans—even as she continued to work as a physician. Medical-thriller master Robin Cook has also kept up his Boston medical practice while churning out a new book almost every year since he wrote *Coma* (1977) during a medical residency. But his first book, 1972's *Year of the Intern*, was written onboard a U.S. Navy research submarine in 75 days.

....

> "Hospital autopsies aren't so bad, because the bodies are very fresh."
>
> —TESS GERRITSEN

....

SECRET AGENT MEN

John le Carré and Ian Fleming are often held up as polar oppo-sites in the spy fiction genre: Le Carré's hero, George Smiley, is a brilliant but physically average agent in a morally complex world, while Fleming's dashing James Bond knocks back cocktails, beds beautiful women, and operates in a world where good and evil are clearly defined. After a glance at their respective creators' resu-més, it's not hard so see why.

Le Carré (the pen name of David John Moore Cornwell) wrote his first book, *Call for the Dead,* while working for British military intelligence (MI5) in West Germany. He later transferred to foreign intelligence (MI6) and wrote *A Murder of Quality* and his best-known novel, *The Spy Who Came in from the Cold.* All three starred world-weary spymaster George Smiley, whose skills were mostly psychological and bureaucratic—an appropriate hero for Le Carré, who claims he spent most of his time in intelligence sitting behind a desk.

In contrast to Le Carré, Ian Fleming came from a life of wealth and privilege (Winston Churchill wrote the obituary for Fleming's father) and had a career in intelligence that wasn't far from the exploits of action hero Bond. In fact, a climactic moment in *Live and Let Die* was inspired by a real-life training exercise, when Fleming had to swim underneath a tanker and attach a mine to it. Fleming worked as assistant to British spymaster Admiral John Godfrey, planning intelligence operations for a commando team named "30 Assault Unit" (30 AU). He later settled in Jamaica in a house he named Goldeneye—after an operation he had planned during World War II.

HAIR OF THE DOG

Bond buffs have ordered their vodka martinis shaken, not stirred, ever since Sean Connery did the same in 1962's *Dr. No*—but they may have been thrown for a loop by the elaborate libation Bond knocked back in 2006's *Casino Royale*. But the recipe for "the Vesper" was taken practically verbatim from the first Bond novel: "Three measures of Gordon's, one of vodka, half a measure of Kina Lillet. Shake it very well until it's ice cold, then add a large thin slice of lemon peel." Later Bond ghostwriter (and legendary drinker) Kingsley Amis remarked that Kina made the Vesper too bitter and recommended Lillet vermouth in its place. And the morning after downing a few Vespers, true Bond fans would no doubt turn to 007's own preferred hangover cure: brandy with club soda and two tablets of phensic (a mixture of aspirin and caffeine).

WORLD'S TOP-EARNING AUTHORS, 2008

Most of them may write "guilty pleasures," but we doubt they feel much guilt about the money they rake in.

Author	Worth (U.S. dollars in millions)
1. J. K. Rowling	$300
2. James Patterson	$50
3. Stephen King	$45
4. Tom Clancy	$35
5. Danielle Steel	$30
6. (tie) John Grisham	$25
6. (tie) Dean Koontz	$25

"He loves cooking—he's done the Cordon Bleu exams—and it's great fun to sit with him in the kitchen while he prepares a meal and see that he's as happy as a clam."

—LITERARY AGENT MORT JANKLOW,
ON HANNIBAL LECTOR CREATOR THOMAS HARRIS

LEGAL EAGLES

Courtroom-thriller masters John Grisham and Scott Turow really are lawyers (though Grisham is retired), but please don't make them the butt of any lawyer jokes: Both men have used their considerable success and legal skills to do some truly good work. One of Turow's highest-profile cases occurred in 1995 when he represented Alejandro Hernandez, who was ultimately released from death row after serving 11 years for a crime he didn't commit. Grisham has churned out one novel almost every year since 1989 but also serves on the board of The Innocence Project, a national organization dedicated to reforming the criminal justice system and exonerating people falsely convicted of crimes. Ironically, he was sued in 2007 for his nonfiction book *The Innocent Man* (about two men falsely accused of murder) by the attorney who prosecuted the case Grisham described.

ROMANCING THE TOME

For someone who wrote only six novels—and was credited anonymously as "A Lady" on the books' title pages—Jane Austen left her mark not only on romantic literature but on literature in general. Just as Bridget Jones owes a debt of personality to Elizabeth Bennet, so do most characters envisioned in what we today call romance novels. Jane Austen didn't live in an era in which Fitzwilliam Darcy could appear bare chested on the cover of a paperback, but she did lay the groundwork for thousands of bodice rippers to come—and the basis for Fabio's career, we suppose.

Any romance fan also owes a debt of gratitude to Harlequin, the pioneering publisher of bodice rippers everywhere. The 60-year-old Toronto-based company—whose titles spend hundreds of weeks on best-seller lists annually—brought the romance novel to new audiences and popular heights in the early 1970s. Booksellers had shied away from selling the mass-market paperbacks, so Harlequin put the books on shelves in supermarkets and drugstores, where their potential readers were more likely to see them.

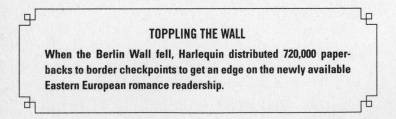

TOPPLING THE WALL

When the Berlin Wall fell, Harlequin distributed 720,000 paperbacks to border checkpoints to get an edge on the newly available Eastern European romance readership.

LUSTY LADIES

If romance novelists write fiction, why do their own lives some-times seem more salacious than their latest plotlines?

Danielle Steel, author of more than 60 novels, is pretty familiar with the *New York Times* best-seller list, appearing on it, with one romantic tome or another, for years at a stretch (381 consecutive weeks, at one point, earning her place-ment in the *Guinness Book of World Records*.) Married (and divorced) five times—twice to convicted felons—the mother of five (and stepmother to two) has at least a few books' worth of material from her own life.

Steel's scandalous personal life was made only worse by her fame as an author. An unauthorized 1993 biography revealed, among other details, that one of her sons had a different biological father (husband No. 3) than most of the family thought (current husband, No. 4). Steel sued the book's writers futilely, then blamed the stress of the situation on the later failure of that marriage. However, she did get another book out of it—the plot of *Malice* shows how tabloid gossip destroys her characters' happy marriage.

Grace Metalious's novel, *Peyton Place,* which revealed the sex and scandal lurking in the shadows of a fictional New England town, was based on a true story of small-town intrigue and caused some scandals of its own. Metalious based one of *Peyton Place's* seamy secrets on the story of a local New England girl who had killed her father after years of sexual abuse and buried him in a barnyard pen.

After *Peyton Place* was published, Metalious's neighbors and fellow townspeople recognized other similar characters and plots in her melodramatic novel. Tomas Makris, who worked with Metalious's husband at the local school, went so far as to sue the author for libel, claiming the character Michael Kyros was based on him. An out-of-court settlement for $60,000 was agreed to, but later editions of the book had to rename the character—the seductive Michael Kyros was rechristened Michael Rossi.

Nora Roberts, the best-selling author of more than 100 romance novels—and mysteries, under the pseudonym J. D. Robb—partially blames her divorce on the initial fame that came with becoming a writer. In Roberts-like fashion, though, things worked out in the end. She ended up getting married again, to the carpenter who came to build her new bookshelves—presumably to hold the hundreds of best sellers she would later publish.

In an incident that certainly didn't do anything to dissuade critics who think that romance novels are all the same, Nora Roberts accused Janet Dailey—herself the author of more than 90 romance novels—of replicating more than a dozen of Roberts's passages in her work. The plagiarism allegations, which Roberts melodramatically labeled "mind rape," were scattered throughout several of Dailey's novels. The lawsuit was settled out of court in 1998 for an undisclosed sum, and Dailey—a friend of Roberts's before the falling out—said in a statement that the "essentially random and nonpervasive acts of copying are attributable to a psychological problem that I never even suspected I had."

THANKS, BUT NO THANKS

Long before her successful newspaper column was adapted to become the best-selling novel *Bridget Jones's Diary,* Helen Fielding tried her hand at traditional romance writing and was summarily rejected by one of Harlequin's U.K. imprints.

MR. RIGHT

Mr. Romance—a reality show on the Oxygen Network, produced by Gene Simmons (yes, the serpent-tongued bass player from KISS)—sought to find Harlequin's next face (and naked chest) of romance in 2005. New Jersey truck driver Randy Ritchwood won the steamy title. No word on whether Simmons tried to enter himself in the running.

....

"Her books were put down by most critics, but readers would not put down her books."

—TODAY SHOW CRITIC GENE SHALIT
EULOGIZING *VALLEY OF THE DOLLS* (1966)
AUTHOR JACQUELINE SUSANN

....

IT'S CRIMINAL

The great detectives of fiction—Sherlock Holmes, Philip Marlowe, Easy Rawlins—all possess character flaws, from arrogance to alcoholism. Perhaps flaws are necessary for the creators of crime fiction, too. How else would they be able to imagine the devious twists and turns that are so important to their stories?

CRIMINAL MINDSET

Though widely considered a master of horror, Edgar Allan Poe (1809–49) is also credited with the creation of the now ubiquitous "detective story" with his short story, "The Murders in the Rue Morgue" (1841). That investigation into the deaths of a mother and daughter also introduced C. August Dupin—widely considered the first detective in fiction—and the familiar tropes of the unwitting sidekick-narrator and mostly clueless police investigators.

NEVER MORE

It's unlikely that Poe borrowed much from his own life for "Rue Morgue," if only because people in 19th-century America were rarely exposed to straight-razor wielding "Ourang-Outangs" (that's orangutan in our 21st-century vernacular). Much has been written about Poe's own troubles, especially his reported alcoholism. And as a West Point cadet, Poe was court-martialed and charged with gross neglect of duty and disobeying orders. Found guilty on all counts, he was kicked out of the Army in 1831. Poe's personal life also tended toward the nefarious. He married his 13-year-old cousin, Virginia Eliza Clemm, in 1836 (though she was listed as 21 years old on the marriage registration); the 27-year-old Poe was more than double her age.

....

*"No doubt you think that you are complimenting me
in comparing me to Dupin," he observed. "Now, in
my opinion, Dupin was a very inferior fellow."*

—SHERLOCK HOLMES,
IN SIR ARTHUR CONAN DOYLE'S *A STUDY IN SCARLET* (1887)

....

NARCOTICS, MY DEAR MAN

Characteristically, Sherlock Holmes thought himself superior to the brilliant Dupin. But his habits leave some doubt in the reader's mind. Sir Arthur Conan Doyle (1859–1930), as narrator Dr. Watson, often wrote of iconic investigator Sherlock Holmes's drug use, especially his injections of "cocaine, a seven percent solution." Watson's response to Holmes's drug use—legal at the time and generally considered harmless—is more prescient than Holmes's sharply honed investigation skills. Dr. Watson describes making valiant efforts to wean Holmes off drugs in the short story "The Adventure of the Missing Three-Quarter" (1904). In the manner of a latter-day Narcotics Anonymous pamphlet, he speaks of how, even off drugs, Holmes's habit "was not dead, but sleeping."

MISQUOTED

Sherlock Holmes's presumed catchphrase, "Elementary, my dear Watson," is not actually uttered by Holmes in any of Conan Doyle's stories. The nearest dialogue is from the short story "The Crooked Man" (1893):
"Excellent!" I cried.
"Elementary," said he.

BLESSING IN DISGUISE?

Actor Alec Guinness claimed that he converted to Catholicism in part because of his experiences playing G. K. Chesterton's (1874–1936) priest-detective Father Brown in the eponymous film.

THE CASE OF THE DISAPPEARING AUTHOR

Agatha Christie's imagination seemed to get the best of her when she abruptly disappeared from her Berkshire, England, home in 1926. Christie (1890–1976), at the time, was reeling from her mother's death and the news that her husband was being unfaithful. For 11 days Christie fans speculated over her disappearance, theorizing that her adulterous husband had murdered her or that she had drowned herself; others conjectured that it was merely a publicity stunt. Sir Arthur Conan Doyle even took one of her gloves to a medium.

Christie, the creator of beloved detectives Miss Marple and Hercule Poirot and the best-selling author of all-time, was found at a health spa. She had registered as South African tourist Teresa Neele (borrowing the surname from her husband's mistress). Perhaps Christie was exacting revenge on her husband, or as more recently theorized, was genuinely in a fugue state—a psychogenic trance. But Christie never explained her disappearance and omitted the episode from her autobiography altogether. Frankly, Miss Marple would never have left the mystery unsolved.

HARD-BOILING OVER

The innovation of mystery-specific pulp magazines in the early 20th century introduced the now familiar—and sometimes

cliché—hard-boiled private investigator, which is usually credited to Carroll John Daly. But it was Sam Spade, a creation of
Dashiell Hammett (1894–1961) in a serial (1929–30) for *Black
Mask,* who became the prototype for the street-savvy, hard-and-
shifty private eye. Spade wasn't above sullying himself by sleeping
with his partner's wife, but he adhered to his own indistinct yet
stringent moral code, as would be the case with some of these
later hard-boiled gumshoes:

- Philip Marlowe, introduced to the detective canon by
  Raymond Chandler, shares many of the characteristics of
  earlier hardened private investigators, with his enthusiasm
  for women and whiskey and a tendency toward talking
  back (for which he was fired from his job with the Los
  Angeles district attorney). Chandler's own job history was
  just as colorful—before he began writing short stories for
  Black Mask, he was fired for absenteeism and on-the-job
  drunkenness from his work as a Los Angeles oil company
  executive. His first novel, *The Big Sleep* (1939), wasn't
  published until Chandler was 51 years old.

- Best known for creating Perry Mason, Erle Stanley Gard-
  ner (under the pseudonym A. A. Fair) also created one
  of the first female private eyes in the hard-boiled genre,
  Bertha Cool, in 1939. A 200-pound widow eschewing the
  Miss Marple tradition for female matron-sleuths, Bertha
  chain-smoked, drank, used profanity, and generally
  behaved like her more notorious male counterparts.

- Hoping to earn enough for a down payment on a house,
  Mickey Spillane (1918–2006) wrote *I, the Jury* (1947) in
  just three weeks, introducing Mike Hammer—the macho,
  ultraviolent private dick—to the world. Of all of the

hard-boiled gumshoes, Hammer probably racked up the highest body count. In his mind, solving the crime meant eye-for-an-eye justice, carried out by him. In the first five Hammer books alone, 48 people are killed—34 of them by Mike Hammer, in a lurid, sadistic fashion. Unfortunately for fans of graphic violence, Spillane became a Jehovah's Witness in 1951 and didn't write for more than 10 years after that; his later books were said to lack Hammer's signature panache for the art of maiming and killing.

- Matthew Scudder, the ex-NYPD detective created by Lawrence Block (1938–) in 1976, is more flawed than most—he is introduced as an alcoholic who accidentally shot a little girl, quit the police force, and abandoned his family. Though Scudder joins Alcoholics Anonymous in later books, Block himself nominated his character as the most overrated fictional detective when asked by *American Heritage* magazine in 2000:

  I'll tell you, if I were going to hire a private eye, Scudder's the last one I'd pick. He's either drunk or going to AA meetings, which leaves him with precious little time for work. His girlfriend's a hooker, and his best buddy is a career criminal and multiple murderer. And he does weird things: In one book he clears his client of a murder the man really did commit, then frames him for one he didn't have anything to do with. Who in his right mind would have anything to do with a guy like that?

THE SINCEREST FORM OF FLATTERY

Before he created Spenser or Jesse Stone, prolific crime author Robert B. Parker (1932–) wrote his 1971 Ph.D. dissertation on the private detectives depicted by Dashiell Hammett, Raymond Chandler, and Ross Macdonald. Less than two decades later, he published *Poodle Springs* (1989), adapted from an unfinished manuscript of Chandler's, and *Perchance to Dream* (1991), a sequel to Chandler's *The Big Sleep*.

GOOD ADVICE

Western and detective novel author Elmore Leonard (1925–) contributed his rules on writing to the *New York Times* in 2001. His sensible advice included: "Never open a book with weather," and "Never use a verb other than 'said' to carry dialogue" (and never modify said with an adverb). On exclamation points: "No more than two or three per 100,000 words of prose."

> "The weapon should always be appropriate to the murderer. For example, elderly ladies, however murderous, are unlikely in the U.K. to have access to guns."
>
> —P. D. James

THE BAD AND THE UGLY

Of course, even as we appreciate oft-maligned genres and writers, there are some that deserve praise for work that is so very bad that it's good. Endorsed by writers no less esteemed than Aldous Huxley and Mark Twain, Irish writer Amanda McKittrick Ros's texts were so purple, it was as though they had been beaten to a bruising by a bad-writing stick. (And that sentence is in tribute to her.)

KEEP A STRAIGHT FACE

The alliteration-adoring Amanda McKittrick Ros (1860–1939) was so famous for her corpulent prose and poetry that J. R. R. Tolkien and C. S. Lewis competed against each other to see who could read the most without laughing. How bad was it? Read this verse and decide for yourself:

> *Beneath me here in stinking clumps*
> *Lies Lawyer Largebones, all in lumps;*
> *A rotten mass of clockholed clay,*
> *Which grown more honeycombed each day.*
> *See how the rats have scratched his face?*
> *Now so unlike the human race;*
> *I very much regret I can't*
> *Assist them in their eager 'bent'*

Americans can claim one of the world's worst writers as their own, too—one so beloved that independent publishing house McSweeney's in 2005 decided to reprint one of his works, *The Riddle of the Traveling Skull,* just to make the world aware of its sheer awfulness. Often referred to as the Ed Wood of detective fiction, Harry Stephen Keeler (1890–1967) wrote *Traveling Skull* and other titles that practically beg you not to read them: *The Man with the Magic Eardrums, Finger! Finger!*, and *The Case of the Transposed Legs*. Not convinced? Keeler writes in the *The Steeltown Strangler*:

> ...We can eat up-town at an air-cooler place—rather half-way deluxe, too, for a town like this—or we can eat at a joint outside the gates where a hundred sweat-encrusted mill-workers, every one with a peeled garlic bean laid alongside his plate, will inhale soup like the roar of 40 Niagras, and crunch victuals like a half-hundred concrete mixers all running at once.

You have to give Keeler a hand for his creativity, though. In *X. Jones, of Scotland Yard*, the main suspect is a killer midget (disguised as a baby, naturally) that stalks his victims in a helicopter. He is known as "the Flying Strangler-Baby."

THE WORST FIRST

In the tradition of "It was a dark and stormy night..." the Bulwer-Lytton Fiction Contest, sponsored by San Jose State University has challenged writers to construct the worst possible first sentence for a novel since 1983. Here are some of our favorite winners:

- The lovely woman-child Kaa was mercilessly chained to the cruel post of the warrior-chief Beast, with his barbarous tribe now stacking wood at her nubile feet, when the strong, clear voice of the poetic and heroic Handsomas roared, "Flick your Bic, crisp that chick, and you'll feel my steel through your last meal."
  —Steven Garman, Pensacola, Florida (1984)

- The countdown had stalled at T minus 69 seconds when Desiree, the first female ape to go up in space, winked at me slyly and pouted her thick, rubbery lips unmistakably—the first of many such advances during what would prove to be the longest, and most memorable, space voyage of my career. —Martha Simpson, Glastonbury, Connecticut (1985)

• She wasn't really my type, a hard-looking but untalented reporter from the local cat box liner, but the first second that the third-rate representative of the fourth estate cracked open a new fifth of old Scotch, my sixth sense said seventh heaven was as close as an eighth note from Beethoven's Ninth Symphony, so, nervous as a tenth grader drowning in eleventh-hour cramming for a physics exam, I swept her into my longing arms, and, humming "The Twelfth of Never," I got lucky on Friday the thirteenth. —Wm. W. "Buddy" Ocheltree, Port Townsend, Washington (1993)

• Paul Revere had just discovered that someone in Boston was a spy for the British, and when he saw the young woman believed to be the spy's girlfriend in an Italian restaurant he said to the waiter, "Hold the spumoni— I'm going to follow the chick an' catch a Tory." —John L. Ashman, Houston, Texas (1995)

• She resolved to end the love affair with Ramon tonight...summarily, like Martha Stewart ripping the sand vein out of a shrimp's tail...though the term "love affair" now struck her as a ridiculous euphemism...not unlike "sand vein," which is after all an intestine, not a vein...and that tarry substance inside certainly isn't sand...and that brought her back to Ramon. —Dave Zobel, Manhattan Beach, California (2004)

BETTER LEFT UNSAID

Samuel Wesley may have been a clergyman by trade (and his sons John and Charles Wesley would later be credited with founding the Methodist movement), but you can't say that he was a stereotypical dour preacher. At least we hope he wasn't too serious when he composed *Maggots: Poems on Several Subjects, Never Before Addressed* (1685). The collection of poems was so resoundingly bad that for more than a century afterward, certain kinds of terrible writing were referred to as "maggoty." Just how bad was it? Judge for yourself; his poems' titles included:

- "On two Souldiers killing one another for a Groat"

- "A Dialogue, Between Chamber-pot and Frying Pan"

- "On a Supper of a Stinking Ducks"

- "An Anacreontique on a Pair of Breeches"

- "A Tame Snake, left in a Box of Bran"

- "A Pindarique, on the Grunting of a Hog"

LIKE PULLING TEETH

Referred to in his day as the "poet laureate of dentistry," Solyman Brown published "Dentalogia, a Poem on the Diseases of the Teeth," in 1833. Perhaps the only epic poem on the subject of dental hygiene, the surprisingly well-received volume was 54 pages long.

YOUNG AT HEART

From Winnie the Pooh to Nancy Drew, your favorite children's characters—and their creators—were often more complex than they seemed. Which universally beloved writer and illustrator moonlighted as a propagandist for the U.S. Army? Which renowned "authors" were really pseudonyms for a virtual army of anonymous writers? Which fairy tale originally ended not with a happily-ever-after wedding but with a 300-year curse on a dead girl? Revisit some of those old favorites that you thought you knew from cover to cover.

GRUESOMELY EVER AFTER

If you've ever revisited one of your favorite childhood stories as an adult, you've probably noticed that the story seems...different. (We're looking at you, *The Lorax!*) There are nuances you missed as a child, details you've forgotten, and things that just may not have been in the edition you owned back then.

This is especially true with traditional stories that are adapted year after year: Sometimes the stories change to match shifting generational attitudes, and other times they are simplified to keep an animated feature film under 90 minutes long. These bowdlerized adaptations are so ubiquitous that the original versions of some of the world's most cherished children's tales, such as *Snow White* and *Cinderella,* are completely unfamiliar—and more disturbing—than you might ever imagine.

THE BROTHERS GRIMM

Brothers Jacob (1785–1863) and Wilhelm (1786–1859) Grimm created collections of popular European myths, legends, and folklore in their native German. Their volumes of fairy tales introduced characters that became familiar to children in every subsequent generation. Many of their stories were later adapted to animated films, from *Snow White* to *Hansel and Gretel,* but the Grimms' stories have more in common with modern horror films than Disney cartoons.

Snow White: The Grimms' version is full of twisted detail. Snow White is exiled by her evil stepmother, the Queen, who commands a hunter to kill Snow White and bring her heart back as proof. Taking pity on her, the hunter brings the Queen the heart of a bear instead—which she eats. The Queen is repaid violently at the end of the tale, when she is forced to dance in red-hot iron slippers until she dies.

Cinderella: The cruel stepsisters—who cut off parts of their own feet in an attempt to trick the prince and fit into the golden (that's right: golden, not glass) slipper—are gruesomely killed at Cinderella's wedding. In a different Grimm edition, they are allowed to live...but charmed pigeons use their beaks to poke out the sisters' eyes, cursing them with blindness.

Rumpelstiltskin: After his plot is foiled, the title character stomps his foot on the ground in a fit of rage, burying his body up to his waist. When he tries to extricate himself, he tears himself in half.

THE OTHERS GRIM

The Grimms' grim imaginings aside, there are a lot of other dark stories out there—tales that many parents would think twice about reading to their children before bedtime.

Pinocchio: This story was first imagined in Carlo Collodi's (1826–90) *The Adventures of Pinocchio* (1883). Most remember the animated Disney feature best, with the delightful Jiminy Cricket, some darkness inside the belly of a whale, and its pro-truth (and anti-big-nose) morality. Collodi's fairy tale, on the other hand, opens with Pinocchio yelping in pain as he's being carved and sanded. He then proceeds to get Geppetto arrested and kills the talking cricket by throwing a hammer at it—all by the end of Chapter 4.

The Little Mermaid: Hans Christian Andersen (1805–75) also had an aversion to the "happily ever after." The Disney adaptation of *The Little Mermaid* was wrapped up with a happy ending, but in Andersen's 1837 version, the little mermaid is forced to watch the prince she loves marry another woman. The sea witch gives her a choice: Stab the prince to death in his sleep or die herself. So, logically, she throws her now-finless self into the sea and, in keeping with the Victorian-era moralizing of so many contemporary fairy tales, will eventually be able to earn her soul back by doing good deeds for 300 years. Maybe.

THE KID-GLOVE TREATMENT

Nathaniel Hawthorne's *The Scarlet Letter* is usually not assigned to students until they are old enough to understand what exactly that scarlet "A" stands for. But 19th-century readers were introduced to Hawthorne at much younger ages—not via bowdlerized (see page 39) editions of *The House of Seven Gables* or *The Scarlet Letter*, but in a handful of children's books, which he wrote both before and after his successful novels were published. Several of the books retold Greek myths and legends in the voice of a young college student entertaining his cousins; another tells the childhood stories of notable figures such as Isaac Newton, Benjamin Franklin, and Oliver Cromwell. Though Hawthorne tried not to, in his words, "write downward" to children, the themes of his children's books were quite different. As Hawthorne wrote in the introduction to his *Biographical Stories for Children,* "The author regards children as sacred, and would not, for the world, cast anything into the fountain of a young heart that might imbitter [sic] and pollute its waters."

SHORT BUT NOT SO SWEET

Of course, traditional children's reading material isn't always a complete story—sometimes it's just a few verses. *Mother Goose's Melodies* (published in the United States in various editions by the early 19th century) catalogued familiar nursery rhymes with origins reaching back hundreds of years.

Those origins weren't necessarily pretty, no matter how catchy the sing-song rhyme scheme or how adorable the accompanying pantomime. The theory that "Ring a Ring o' Roses" (or "Ring Around the Rosie") was about the bubonic plague has been debunked by many historians, but many "innocent" rhymes really were inspired by sordid or grotesque events in history. If you're reading a rhyme for the umpteenth time, it's more fun to imagine that some of the content may not be suitable for minor children.

"Mary, Mary, Quite Contrary"
Mary, Mary, quite contrary,
How does your garden grow?
With silver bells and cockleshells
And pretty maids all in a row.

"Mary" is thought to be Bloody Mary (Queen Mary I), who executed hundreds of Protestant dissenters. The "silver bells and cockleshells" are thought to be implements of torture: thumbscrews and genital clamps. And those pretty maids? Probably a reference to the "Scottish maiden," an early guillotine.

"Georgie Porgie"
Georgie Porgie pudding and pie
Kissed the girls and made them cry
When the boys came out to play
Georgie Porgie ran away.

More royal hijinks: Historians believe that "Georgie" refers to George Villiers, First Duke of Buckingham and rumored homosexual, whom King James I honored as "Gentleman of the Bedchamber" until a disapproving Parliament "came out to play."

"Jack and Jill"
Jack and Jill went up the hill
To fetch a pail of water.
Jack fell down and broke his crown,
And Jill came tumbling after.

These origins are quite disputed, but one hypothesis is that "Jack and Jill" refers to King Louis XVI and his wife, Marie Antoinette. The guillotine undoubtedly broke Louis XVI's crown (and Marie Antoinette's shortly thereafter).

LIONS AND TIGERS AND BEARS (OH MY!)

Furry and feathered friends have always had a place in our favorite stories. For every Alice (in Wonderland) and Dorothy (of Kansas), there's a Cheshire Cat or a Toto. These mostly four-legged creatures have many of the same quirks as their two-legged counterparts in fiction, but the idea of a toad driving a motorcar or a monkey taking the subway to his job as a window washer is somehow infinitely more appealing.

Most writers didn't just pull their anthropomorphized creatures out of thin air. Some of their real-life inspirations almost served in World War I, some were born out of annoyance with older relatives, and some were based on the author's own children.

EXOTIC LEADING CREATURES

Some Pig: E. B. White may often be remembered as a cosmopolitan *New Yorker* writer, but his children's books showed an affinity for the animal kingdom that went beyond the Central Park Zoo. Most fans of the original porcine leading man, Wilbur in *Charlotte's Web* (1952), believe that the tale was in part a natural continuation of White's 1948 essay "Death of a Pig." White had tried, unsuccessfully, to save a pig (originally purchased to be eaten) from an illness. "I found myself cast suddenly in the role of pig's friend and physician—a farcical character with an enema bag for a prop," he wrote. The pig didn't make it to White's dinner table that winter.

Monkey See, Monkey Do: H. A. (Hans Augusto) Rey and Margret Rey, both German-born Jews, married in Brazil in 1935 and sailed to Europe for a honeymoon, bringing their two pet marmoset monkeys along with them. Unfortunately, the sweaters Margret had knit for the simian twosome were not warm enough, and they died during the voyage. The Reys settled in Paris and signed a contract in 1939 with a French publisher for *The Adventures of Fifi*—a book about a troublemaking monkey. With the manuscript, they escaped wartime Paris ahead of approaching Nazi soldiers and sailed to New York in 1940. There "Fifi" became "Curious George": The American publisher believed that no mischievous male monkey should be named Fifi.

A PARTICULARLY PORCINE PROBLEM

William Steig used lots of anthropomorphized animals in his children's books, which included *Shrek!* (1990) and *Doctor De Soto* (1982)—the latter about a mouse-dentist who treats (and tricks) a fox with a toothache. But another animal selection landed him in hot water in 1970, when he was boycotted by the International Conference of Police Associations because his book *Sylvester and the Magic Pebble* (1969) depicted police officers as pigs.

Grin and Bear It: Winnie—short for Winnipeg—the Pooh was a brave Canadian soldier, of sorts, during World War I. Purchased for $20, the black bear cub was adopted as a mascot by a Canadian infantry brigade and traveled with the soldiers to England. While the infantry was fighting in mainland Europe, Winnie was left in the London Zoo, where he became a favorite attraction. One of his frequent visitors was A. A. Milne's son, Christopher Robin Milne. Christopher Robin's interactions with his toys—which included a teddy bear, a tiger, a pig, a baby kangaroo, and a donkey with no tail—became the basis for Milne's stories.

A Monster in the Family: Maurice Sendak had intended to create wild horses for a new book, originally titled *Where the Wild Horses Are*. But he quickly became frustrated with how difficult horses were to draw. So he began drawing monsters—griffins, gargoyles, and other creatures. But the monsters became satisfying to him only when he turned them into caricatures of his uncles and aunts, whom he so disliked as a child, because "they were rude, and because they ruined every Sunday, and because they ate all our food."

Toad in a Hole: The inspiration for Disneyland's "Mr. Toad's Wild Ride" attraction, Toad of Toad Hall in *Wind in the Willows* (1908), came out of a series of letters that author Kenneth Grahame wrote to his son Alastair, who was possibly as unruly as Toad. Alastair was a disobedient child, known to attack other children in London's Kensington Gardens or to lie down in front of traffic, forcing cars to stop.

FINDING INSPIRATION IN DARKNESS

The Dementors introduced in *Harry Potter and the Prisoner of Azkaban* (1999)—hooded creatures that feed on human happiness—were inspired by J. K. Rowling's bout with clinical depression following the birth of her daughter.

Not So Cuddly Bunny: With his wife, Debbie, James Howe began writing *Bunnicula*—the story of a stealthy, vegetarian vampire rabbit—in the late 1970s. The couple was inspired by their longtime devotion to vampire movies on late-night TV, which they considered more silly than scary. "It came from asking the question, what's the silliest, least likely vampire I can imagine?" Howe said.

IT'S RAINING CATS AND DOGS
(AND OTHER PETS AND PESTS)

A miscellany of tidbits about our most beloved—or loathed—animal characters and their creators.

Clifford the Big Red Dog (1963), Norman Bridwell	Named after Bridwell's wife's childhood imaginary friend, Clifford was imagined as a giant dog like the one Bridwell himself had wanted as a child (he wanted to be able to ride it).
The Incredible Journey (1961), Sheila Burnford	Burnford didn't intend for her story to become a children's book; her animals don't speak. A human narrator follows two dogs and a Siamese cat (who hates cats) on their trip through northwestern Ontario in search of their masters.
The Cat in the Hat (1957), Dr. Seuss	Dr. Seuss (Theodor Geisel) was attempting to create a book that would be accessible to beginning readers. He whittled a list of 400 early vocabulary words down to 223, adding 13 additional words. "Cat" and "Hat" were the first two rhyming words on the list.
The Poky Little Puppy (1942), Gustaf Tenggren, illustrator	One of the first Little Golden Books, *The Poky Little Puppy* is one of the best-selling children's picture books of all time. Tenggren was also a successful animator who had worked on Disney classics such as *Bambi, Snow White and the Seven Dwarfs,* and *Fantasia.*

> "She will probably be played by a boy, if one
> clever enough can be found, and must never be
> on two legs except on those rare occasions when
> an ordinary nurse would be on four."

> —J. M. BARRIE (STAGE DIRECTION FOR NANA,
> THE DARLINGS' NURSEMAID, IN PETER PAN)

BACK IN THE USSR

Robert McCloskey's Caldecott award–winning *Make Way for Ducklings* (1941) chronicled the march of Mrs. Mallard and her eight ducklings from their birthplace, an island in Boston's Charles River, to their new home in Boston's Public Garden, assisted by kindly police officers. (McCloskey's duckling illustrations owed their realism to six live duckling models he had living in his studio at the time.) Mrs. Mallard and the ducklings made the move to the Public Garden permanent when they were immortalized in bronze on cobblestones by sculptor Nancy Schön in a life-sized statue installed there in 1987.

A replica of the "Ducklings" statue also played a minor role in ending the cold war. On the occasion of the START treaty signing in 1991, Barbara Bush presented the statue to Raisa Gorbachev as a gift "given in love and friendship to the children of the Soviet Union, on behalf of the children of the United States."

TELL ME A STORY

Many "children's" authors didn't *always* limit themselves to writing at a fifth-grade reading level. Whether they were writing songs about venereal disease, illustrating manuals for orgasmic-energy machines, or penning tales about murderous, meat-wielding wives, one thing is for certain: Some of your favorite children's authors churned out plenty of work that is not for underaged eyes.

SISTER, CAN YOU SPARE A DIME?

Louisa May Alcott (1832–88) first began making money as a writer by publishing stories in magazines and newspapers—much like her fictional *Little Women* counterpart, Jo March—though none of the publication titles were so cuttingly named as March's *Daily Volcano*. Alcott's stories were as full of wily heroines, sexual intrigue, and pure evil as the era allowed. These tall tales were published anonymously, but dozens of stories are attributed to her now. "Pauline's Passion and Punishment," "Behind a Mask, or A Woman's Power," and "Betrayed by a Buckle," among others, bear witness to the purplish prose that put food on her family's table during their lean years. (Her transcendentalist-philosopher father had once returned from a long lecture tour with a mere dollar in earnings.) In her own words, Alcott was "the goose that laid the golden egg," but she was curiously as contemptuous of her bestselling novels as she was of the thrillers, calling *Little Women* "moral pap for the young."

ALTERNATIVE ENERGY

Shrek! creator William Steig (1907–2003) may be remembered best for his children's books, but he didn't even start illustrating for children until he was in his 60s. Steig was a well-known *New Yorker* cartoonist for years and, later in life, said that he turned to children's books only to avoid having to supplement his income by drawing advertisements. Steig's strangest illustrations, though, are probably those found in psychoanalyst Wilhelm Reich's *Listen, Little Man!* Reich was the creator of "orgone therapy," which promised to harness orgasmic energy. Steig was a great believer in Reich's theories and even dedicated a book to him; he sat in his orgone box—a telephone booth–like structure made of cardboard, wire, and metal—daily for most of his life.

IN THE ARMY NOW

Readers of Dr. Seuss's work (or, more accurately, their parents) have long identified political allegory in his children's books, from *How the Grinch Stole Christmas* (materialism) to *The Butter Battle Book* (nuclear proliferation). It's probably no surprise to those on-the-ball readers that Theodor Geisel also penned political cartoons in the years surrounding World War II—and spent several years during the war making propaganda films for the U.S. Army.

SHEL SHOCKED

Shel Silverstein (1932–99) fans usually cite his poetry collections, *Where the Sidewalk Ends* and *A Light in the Attic,* or his children's story, *The Giving Tree,* as favorites. But only a superfan would know to read those books while listening to Johnny Cash sing "A Boy Named Sue"—the song for which Silverstein won a songwriting Grammy. Silverstein also wrote other popular songs, including "The Cover of the Rolling Stone" and "Don't Give a Dose to the One You Love the Most" (a song about venereal disease) for Dr. Hook & the Medicine

Show. Silverstein's randiness wasn't limited to songwriting either: His illustrations have appeared in *Playboy* and his "Buy One, Get One Free," a short-sketch play, featured two prostitutes making their sales pitch entirely in rhyme.

RATED R

Long before the success of *Charlie and the Chocolate Factory* (1964), Roald Dahl's earliest writing appeared in the pages of *Playboy* and in other adult magazines. In fact, Dahl didn't even begin writing for children until he had children of his own to write for. From the twisted title story in *Switch Bitch* to "Lamb to the Slaughter"—a tale about a woman who kills her husband by beating him with a frozen leg of lamb, which she then serves to the detectives that come to investigate—Dahl's short stories are definitely not anything you'd read to a child before bedtime, unless you were trying to give him nightmares.

....

"I'm probably more pleased with my children's books than with my adult short stories. Children's books are harder to write. It's tougher to keep a child interested, because a child doesn't have the concentration of an adult. A child knows the television is in the next room. It's tough to hold a child, but it's a lovely thing to try to do."

—ROALD DAHL

....

"You cannot write for children... They're much too complicated. You can only write books that are of interest to them."

—Maurice Sendak

LONGSTOCKING LAWS

Astrid Lindgren's (1907–2002) free-spirited Pippi Longstocking (Pippilotta Delicatessa Windowshade Mackrelmint Efraim's Daughter Longstocking, to be exact) may have thought Lindgren became a little too serious in later years. The Swedish writer sparked controversy in 1976 when a newspaper published her satirical adult fairy tale "Pomperipossa in the World of Money." The story protested the marginal tax rate for self-employed artists, which had ballooned to an impossible-seeming 102 percent (the artist was required to pay payroll taxes and employer's fees). She also wielded her pen as a political sword in protest of the treatment of farm animals: "Every pig is entitled to a happy pig life," said Lindgren in an open letter to the prime minister, published in major Swedish newspapers. A law that ensured farm animals were treated humanely was passed in Sweden in 1988; it was informally named after Lindgren.

HEAL THYSELF

Generations of children will always remember Judith Viorst (1931–) as the author of *Alexander and the Terrible, Horrible, No Good, Very Bad Day*—which she based on her own sons.

But Viorst, a research graduate in psychology, also wrote poetry and nonfiction books—mostly of the self-help variety. In fact, one of her children's books, *The Tenth Good Thing About Barney,* which deals with getting over the death of a pet, could be said to be part of a children's self-help genre if (shudder) there were such a thing.

PART-TIME AUTHOR

The first time he ever wrote a book for children, Sherman Alexie (1966–) won the National Book Award (2007) for young people's literature. In the semiautobiographical novel *The Absolutely True Diary of a Part-Time Indian,* Alexie wrote about his decision to attend an off-reservation high school, where "he was the only Indian, except for the school mascot." Alexie's other writing, including poetry, short stories, and the celebrated independent film *Smoke Signals,* may also have won him awards, but Alexie was most gratified by the response to *Part-Time Indian,* saying of his book tour, "The response from the road is larger than anything in my career. My wife and I are calling it the hug-and-run tour. People are coming up in tears, and hugging me and running. There is no jaded literary response among the audience. It's so validating."

....

"When I was a kid, I would much rather have been a good baseball player or a hit with the girls. But I couldn't play ball. I couldn't dance. So I started to draw and to write."

—**SHEL SILVERSTEIN**

....

PARENTAL GUIDANCE SUGGESTED

Reading is a good thing for kids, right? Books introduce knowledge and light and new perspectives that open the eyes of our little ones...don't they?

To some, books look more like a threat, chock-full of smut and subversive ideas. The presence of many, many children's books and young adult novels in libraries and classrooms are challenged each year by individuals and parent organizations. If you're thinking that only the worst, most age-inappropriate titles are ever questioned, think again: Even those long-deemed classics by teachers and young readers alike have been thrown off of curricula and plucked from library shelves in towns across North America.

CRITICAL MASS

The Adventures of Huckleberry Finn (1884): No less a writer than Ernest Hemingway flatters Mark Twain's novel as the font of more than a century of literature. But despite its early and frequent placement on English class reading lists, *The Adventures of Huckleberry Finn* may be as talked about outside of classrooms as in them. In a letter written the year after his book's publication, Mark Twain (b. Samuel Clemens, 1835–1910) wrote, "The Committee of the Public Library of Concord, Mass., have given us a rattling tip-top puff which will go into every paper in the country. They have expelled Huck from their library as 'trash and suitable only for the slums.' That will sell 25,000 copies for us sure."

The leading target of literary censorship efforts everywhere, *Huck* remains controversial to this day, mostly due to the language—in keeping with the age—of its racial references. As recently as 2007, it was challenged in schools in Minnesota, Texas, and Connecticut, the latter "because the 'N' word is used in the book 212 times." Let's just hope that they didn't make a student do the counting.

....

"All modern American literature comes from one book by Mark Twain called Huckleberry Finn.... *American writing comes from that. There was nothing before. There has been nothing as good since."*

—ERNEST HEMINGWAY

....

The Catcher in the Rye (1952): J. D. Salinger's young adult classic is another challenged list mainstay. Alienated antihero Holden Caulfield quickly found a place on high school reading lists and just as quickly found his placement challenged by those he would undoubtedly deem phonies. Complaints against the book ranged from antiwhite and obscene in Selinsgrove, PA, in 1975, to violations of the Morris, Manitoba, school libraries' guidelines regarding "excess vulgar language, sexual scenes, things concerning moral issues, excessive violence, and anything dealing with the occult" in 1982. Poor Holden found himself expelled, yet again.

Judy Blume: *Huckleberry Finn* may have the record for longest-running on the banned/challenged books list, but Twain isn't the most-banned author. That dubious honor probably goes to Judy Blume (1938–), who took up five slots (out of 100) on the American Library Association's most recent ranking of banned or challenged books. The *Are You There God? It's Me, Margaret* author has responded to critics by becoming active in anticensorship organizations. In 1999 she published *Places I Never Meant to Be,* a volume of short stories by other well-known children's authors who had seen their work removed from library and classroom shelves, including Katherine Paterson (*Bridge to Terabithia*), Walter Dean Myers (*Fallen Angels*), and Paul Zindel (*The Pigman*).

That same year Blume also rose to defend *Harry Potter* author J. K. Rowling against rising calls for boycotts of the series and upcoming films in a *New York Times* editorial, writing, "At the rate we're going, I can imagine next year's headline: '*Goodnight Moon* Banned for Encouraging Children to Communicate with Furniture.' And we all know where that can lead, don't we?"

PHOTO FINISHED

Judy Blume's jest about Margaret Wise Brown's bedtime classic *Goodnight Moon* (1947) wasn't entirely off the mark. In 2005, Harper Collins made a small but significant change to the book to stop it from sending a potentially "harmful message" to kids. The change? The publisher digitally altered a back-cover photograph of illustrator Clement Hurd—to remove a cigarette that had dangled between his fingers for nearly 60 years.

READ AT YOUR OWN RISK

What's all the fuss about? Here's why some concerned citizens wanted to ban classic books.

Brave New World
(1932), Aldous Huxley

Makes promiscuous sex "look like fun" (1980); centers "around negative activity" and opposes the health curriculum (1993); contains "orgies, self-flogging, suicide" and characters with "contempt for religion, marriage, and the family" (2000).

Of Mice and Men
(1937), John Steinbeck

"Steinbeck is known to have had an antibusiness attitude" and "he was very questionable as to his patriotism" (1989); contains "profane language, moral statement, treatment of the retarded, and the violent ending" (1993); "takes God's name in vain 15 times and uses Jesus's name lightly" (1998).

Lord of the Flies
(1954), William Golding

Is "demoralizing inasmuch as it implies that man is little more than an animal" (1981).

To Kill a Mockingbird
(1960), Harper Lee

Contains the words damn and whore lady (1977), "profanity and racial slurs" (1985); causes "psychological damages to the positive integration process" and "represents institutionalized racism under the guise of good literature" (1981).

One Flew Over the Cuckoo's Nest
(1962), Ken Kesey

"Glorifies criminal activity, has a tendency to corrupt juveniles and contains descriptions of bestiality, bizarre violence, and torture, dismemberment, death, and human elimination" (1974).

Slaughterhouse-Five
(1969), Kurt Vonnegut

Contains "foul language, a section depicting a picture of an act of bestiality, a reference to 'Magic Fingers' attached to the protagonist's bed to help him sleep, and the sentence: 'The gun made a ripping sound like the opening of the fly of God Almighty'" (1985).

In the Night Kitchen
(1970), Maurice Sendak

"The little boy pictured did not have any clothes on and it pictured his private area" (1994) so the book "could lay the foundation for future use of pornography."

The Golden Compass	The main character drinks wine and ingests poppy with
(1995), Philip Pullman	her meals (Kentucky, 2007); the trilogy is "written by an
	atheist where the characters and text are anti-God, anti-
	Catholic, and antireligion" (Ontario, 2007).

NEWS FLASH: SATAN LOVES HARRY POTTER!

Many of the most zealous *Harry Potter* critics have been fooled by a bizarre story, spread via email, message boards, and blogs, that originated in the satirical newspaper *The Onion*—but was passed around by church and parents' groups who mistook it for factual journalism. The article, *"Harry Potter* Books Spark Rise in Satanism Among Children" appeared just after the fourth volume in the series was published, and contained the publication's signature tongue-in-cheek, AP-style news parody:

> "Harry is an absolute godsend to our cause," said
> High Priest Egan of the First Church of Satan
> in Salem, MA. "An organization like ours thrives
> on new blood—no pun intended—and we've
> had more applicants than we can handle lately.
> And, of course, practically all of them are virgins,
> which is gravy."

....

> *"You have got to be very careful of banning.*
> *What you ban is not going to hurt anybody,*
> *usually. But the act of banning is."*

—MADELEINE L'ENGLE (1918–2007)

....

PARENTAL ADVISORY

After being challenged over its antireligious themes, *The Golden Compass,* the first book in Philip Pullman's frequently challenged His Dark Materials trilogy (see page 101), was allowed to remain in the libraries of a publicly funded Catholic school district in Mississauga, Ontario, in 2008—but with a disclaimer. The district added a sticker to the inside cover of each book, which warned readers that "representations of the church in this novel are purely fictional and are not reflective of the real Roman Catholic Church or the Gospel of Jesus Christ."

TREE'ED OFF

Dr. Seuss (Theodor Geisel) was challenged in Laytonville, CA—redwood territory—in 1989, after logging-equipment wholesaler Bill Bailey's second-grader "came home and labeled [him] a criminal" after reading *The Lorax.* Local residents began buying ads in the local paper in protest, one of which read, "To teach our children that harvesting redwood trees is bad is not the education we need."

"Censorship is telling a man he can't have a steak just because a baby can't chew it."

—MARK TWAIN

NANCY DREW AND HER
MANY MOMMIES

Ever read anything by Mildred Wirt Benson? Harriet Stratemeyer Adams? If you ever read any of Carolyn Keene's original
Nancy Drew novels, you likely have: Adams and Benson were
the primary authors behind the pseudonymous Carolyn Keene.
The not-so-hidden dirty secret behind many children's books
is that the author listed on the front cover—even if he or she
actually exists—may not have written a word of what the reader
finds inside. Whether you grew up on Tom Swift and the Bobbsey
Twins or the Baby-Sitters' Club and Fear Street, the series stayed
the same, but the author rarely did.

The Stratemeyer Syndicate perfected the process of the
ghostwritten children's series in the early 20th century. Syndicate
creator Edward Stratemeyer—who shied away from the idea that
children's books necessarily had to contain moral instruction—
began publishing the Rover Boys series in 1899, followed by Tom
Swift and the Bobbsey Twins. The process of creating the books
evolved into an assembly line process, in which Stratemeyer himself (or someone else at the syndicate) would outline the basic
story and pass it off to a ghostwriter for development. To maintain
the appearance that each book was written by the same author,
Stratemeyer chose a pen name when he created a new series.

Canadian author Leslie McFarlane is thought to have been
primarily responsible for turning the idea of the Hardy Boys
into the behemoth detective series it was to become, writing
at least 20 of the first 25 books credited to Franklin W. Dixon.
McFarlane was initially contracted for the first three books in
the series, which were to be released all at once, in keeping with
Stratemeyer's "breeder" theory: A new series always launched the

first three books at the same time (a practice many book pack-agers continue to this day). Hence, the characterizations in the original series, such as the lovably tough Aunt Gertrude and the clumsy prankster Chet Morton, were all creations of McFarlane. McFarlane, who would go on to work on the TV show *Bonanza* and create more than 50 films for Canada's National Film Board, was paid as little as $85 per book and no more than $165.

EVERYTHING OLD IS NEW AGAIN

Of course, even a beloved series loses its relevance over time. The Hardy Boys books were first given heavy revisions in 1959 to remove dated references to "roadsters" and racially insensitive language and stereotypes. Nancy Drew also received a number of makeovers through the years, as her hair went from blond to "titian"—initially the result of a printer's color error on the cover—to strawberry blond.

Then-syndicate boss and sometime Nancy Drew author Harriet Stratemeyer Adams chafed under the publisher's revision requests, which took place over 20 years beginning in 1959, often writing defensively to Grosset and Dunlap editor Anne Hagan. According to Nancy Drew scholar Jennifer Fisher, Harriet did not find the following comments to be "top-quality editing":

> "Ned is doltish," "McGinnis sounds like a dumb cop,"
> "This is icky," "Nancy sounds like a nasty female." Harriet
> pondered, "Anne, are your remarks intended to mend
> story holes or do you get some sadistic fun out of down-grading and offending me? It will take me a long time
> to live down the remark, 'Nancy sounds like a nasty
> female.'"

SWEET VALLEY'S TUMMY-TUCK

The Sweet Valley High series, starring identical twins Jessica and Elizabeth Wakefield, was given a 21st-century revamp of its own, complete with references to texting and Internet dating. No word yet on whether they'll update the insane plots to make them more in touch with reality, too.

Old Sweet Valley High (c. 1983)	New Sweet Valley High (c. 2008)
Elizabeth and Jessica share a Fiat convertible	The twins tool around in a red Jeep Wrangler
The twins have "perfect size 6 figures"	Elizabeth and Jessica shrunk down to a size 4
Elizabeth writes the "Eyes and Ears" gossip column in the SVH newspaper *The Oracle*	Elizabeth edits the school newspaper website and has a secret blog
Student band "The Droids" plays school dances	"The Droids" are now "Valley of Death"
Attractive boys described as "handsome"	At least two mentions of boys being "Abercrombie-hot"

A "GHOST" NO LONGER

In his salad days, acclaimed fiction writer Tom Perrotta *(Election, Little Children)* was a ghostwriter for R. L. Stine's Fear Street series.

STRANGER THAN FICTION

Sometimes the truth really is strange—and supposedly true stories often turn out to have more than a dash of fiction in the mix. Here we present the true stories behind the most memorable literary hoaxes of all time; surprising facts about memoirists who claim to lay it all on the line; tantalizing private thoughts from the diaries and correspondence of great writers; and essential information about books that truly changed the world.

THE LONG CON

If you're an avid reader (and if you're not, what are you doing here?), you probably know at least a little bit about James Frey— the gritty, compelling, once-Oprah-beloved memoirist—whose down-and-dirty *A Million Little Pieces* turned out to be filled with a million little lies. Frey's fiasco looms large in recent publishing history, but he's far from the first (or the worst) perpetrator of nonfiction fraud. Here we present a rogues' gallery of literary liars through the ages.

WHEN FRAUD IS ALL IN THE FAMILY

Less widely known but far stranger than Frey's debacle is the tale of J. T. LeRoy, whose first published book (*Sarah*, 1999) presented the supposedly semi-autobiographical story of a teen boy whose mother had pimped him as a cross-dressing prostitute at truck stops across America. A cult following had been building around LeRoy for years, but he never appeared in public, and even his agent and editors never met him in person: Interviews were conducted over the phone, and public readings of his work were performed by other people. After *Sarah* hit the shelves, LeRoy started making public appearances, albeit disguised in wigs, hats, and sunglasses—supposedly to help him cope with the near-crippling shyness and insecurity caused by his damaged youth.

But a 2006 *New York Times* exposé (triggered by, of all things, a LeRoy-penned travel story about Disneyland Paris for the *Times'* travel supplement) revealed the bizarre truth: The 25-year-old LeRoy's works were actually written by 40-year-old musician Laura Albert, who had also given all of LeRoy's phone interviews; LeRoy was played in person by Savannah Knoop, the half-sister of

Albert's partner, with Albert always standing nearby pretending to be "Emily," LeRoy's close friend and "outreach worker."

A THOUSAND LITTLE REFUNDS

Despite the controversy over *A Million Little Pieces,* only 1,729 people sought reimbursement for their purchase of Frey's memoir—a total of $27,348 out of the $2.35 million fund created to cover costs related to a class-action lawsuit.

THE (MIS)EDUCATION OF LITTLE TREE

- Forest "Little Tree" Carter's *The Education of Little Tree* (1976) is the inspiring story of a slice of the author's childhood: raised by his Cherokee grandparents, taught a variety of simple lessons about the world and Indian culture, forced into an orphanage where he confronts racism against his people, and eventually rescued. The book sold millions of copies and won the first American Booksellers Association Book of the Year (ABBY) award in 1991—and soon thereafter was proved to be a disturbing fraud. Not only was "Little Tree" Carter a fictional creation, but the true author, Asa Earl Carter, was a former Ku Klux Klan member who had penned Alabama governor George Wallace's hateful speech calling for "Segregation today! Segregation tomorrow! Segregation forever!"

- Some eight years after the truth about *Little Tree* was revealed, another breakout Native American author, known as Nasdijj, appeared in the pages of *Esquire* with the heartrending story of his adopted son, who suffered from fetal alcohol syndrome. The story was a finalist for a National Magazine Award and catapulted Nasdijj to instant literary fame: He wrote three critically acclaimed memoirs over the next five years—but then critics started to notice cultural anachronisms and hints that Nasdijj had cribbed portions of his books from other writers. The writer was eventually unmasked by *LA Weekly* as Lansing, Michigan, native Tim Barrus, previously an author of gay sadomasochistic fiction and coiner of the term leather lit.

- Margaret B. Jones, a half-Native American foster child, claimed to have grown up on the streets of L.A.'s South Central neighborhood and run with the Bloods. Her memoir, *Love and Consequences* (2008) scored a favorable *New York Times* review and a profile in the paper's Home & Garden section—which prompted her sister to call her publisher less than a week later, revealing the truth: Jones was really Margaret Seltzer, a thoroughly white girl who had grown up in upper-class Sherman Oaks, California.

CLOSE ENCOUNTERS OF THE FALSE KIND

Did you know that much modern computer and telecommunications equipment was made possible by alien technology recovered from a 1947 UFO crash near Roswell, New Mexico? Well, then, you must have read retired Army Col. Philip J. Corso's *The Day After Roswell* (1998), which purported to expose long-hidden government secrets about just such an incident. None of it was true, of course, but Corso's military credentials were enough to elicit a complimentary book blurb and foreword from Sen. Strom Thurmond—who thought the book was a straightforward memoir but promptly retracted his foreword when he discovered it was a preposterous story about little green men.

IS IT A "LITERARY" HOAX IF THEY NEVER WROTE THE BOOK?

In 1970, novelist Clifford Irving decided to pitch a biography of reclusive billionaire (and milk-bottle enthusiast) Howard Hughes—despite the fact that Irving had never met the man and had no prospect of doing so. But Irving hooked up with fellow writer Richard Suskind to forge interviews and documents with Hughes's signature and won a $750,000 advance for the project. The book failed to appear, and even Hughes emerged from hiding to condemn the writers, who served jail time.

HOLOCAUST HOAXES

To Thine Own Self Be True: In 1995, *Fragments: Memories of a Wartime Childhood* was published to near-universal acclaim. Binjamin Wilkomirski spilled out a heartrending tale: He was a Latvian Jew whose parents were killed in World War II, leaving him to serve out the rest of the war enduring the horrors of Polish concentration camps— followed by the added indignity of a postwar adoptive family that tried to suppress his memories and change his identity. Published in 12 languages, the book won a 1996 National Jewish Book Award, among others, and Wilkomirski established himself as a respected expert on the Holocaust. By 2000, however, Wilkomirski's story had been thoroughly debunked: He wasn't Jewish *or* Latvian...and had never been in a Nazi death camp; he was born Bruno Grosjean to an unwed mother in 1941, placed in an orphanage, and in 1945 adopted by a well-to-do Swiss family—who left him a substantial inheritance in 1986. Yet Wilkomirski refused to ever admit the fraud, first claiming he had been switched with the "real" Bruno Grosjean, then saying it had been the readers' "choice" to read his book as literature or as a true memoir.

Lying with the Wolves: Wilkomirski's story was fiction, but it was at least plausible. It's less easy to understand how people fell for Misha Defonseca's *Misha: A Mémoire of the Holocaust Years* (1997)—in which the author claimed that while she wandered Europe alone, searching for her Nazi-abducted Jewish parents, she was sheltered by a pack of wolves and stabbed a Nazi soldier. Her parents were really arrested, but that was virtually the only point of truth in the book: Her family was actually Catholic, and Misha spent the entirety of the war in the care of her other relatives.

The (Bad) Apple of His Eye: We're not sure why Oprah seems to attract (or fall for) so many dishonest authors, but she dubbed the tale of Herman Rosenblat "the single greatest love story...we've ever told on the air." Rosenblat claimed that a 9-year-old girl threw apples to him over a concentration camp fence, and decades later they met again on a blind date, fell in love, and were married. Unlike his fellow frauds, Rosenblat did spend time in the Buchenwald concentration camp. But the "hook" of his story, the apples and the "angel at the fence," were revealed as inventions—but not before the story had been made into a children's book, and filming was about to begin on a feature film.

LIVE FAST, DIE YOUNG...

Thomas Chatterton (1752–70), the son of a church sexton, was a creative boy whose writing failed to win any recognition—but when he "discovered" a sheaf of poems written by one Thomas Rowley, a hitherto unknown 15th century priest, he received all the attention he ever wanted and then some. Naturally, Rowley was a complete fiction and the poems were written by Chatterton; he continued to "find" Rowley poems, for which he was paid handsomely, but still yearned to be recognized on his own merits. That day never came, and at age 17, Chatterton wrote one final poem and poisoned himself with arsenic. In a cruel twist, his untimely end brought his own work to the attention of some of the greatest poets of the time: John Keats's *Endymion* is even dedicated to Chatterton.

LIKE FATHER, LIKE SON

William Henry Ireland (1777–1835) inherited an appreciation for old books from his father but also saw that enthusiasts could be easily taken advantage of—as when his gullible, Shakespeare-obsessed father was conned into buying counterfeit artifacts of the Bard. Inspired by earlier literary forgers, including Thomas Chatterton, Ireland embarked at age 17 on an ambitious and startlingly successful scam. William, who worked as a lawyer's apprentice, began collecting blank sheets of parchment from old mortgages and other files, on which he forged a variety of documents—including some with William Shakespeare's signature. After convincing his father that the "found" documents were genuine, young Ireland began churning out and selling a steady stream of forged Shakespearean artifacts: letters (to Anne Hathaway and Queen Elizabeth I), manuscript pages (from

Hamlet and *King Lear*), and even an entirely new play entitled *Vortigern and Rowena*, which opened in 1796 to great fanfare but closed after a single performance. The play was roundly panned in the press, and scholars and critics had already begun to debunk the claim of Shakespearean origin, with many accusing the elder Ireland of staging the hoax. William published a complete confession, but the scandal drove father and son apart, and their family reputation never recovered.

ANGRY PENGUINS AND NOSE-PICKING URCHINS

In 1944, a woman named Ethel Malley sent the manuscript of a long poem sequence entitled *The Darkening Ecliptic*—written by her brother, who had recently died of Graves' disease—to the editor of the Australian avant-garde literary magazine *Angry Penguins*. The editor not only published the poems, he rushed a special edition of the magazine to press, complete with a specially commissioned cover painting and a 3,000-word analysis of Malley's poems. But within a few months, he found himself subject to ridicule when it was revealed that the true authors of "Malley's" poems were James McAuley and Harold Stewart, who had thrown together the entire cycle in a single afternoon, copying random phrases from reference books and Shakespeare's plays, and intentionally choosing "awkward rhymes from a *Ripman's Rhyming Dictionary.*" Their target was the entirety of late-Modern poetry, which they felt had degenerated into incoherence.

Angry Penguins folded (not entirely for reasons related to the Malley scandal) but curiously, "Ern Malley" and his poems have had a lasting, serious impact on the arts in Australia—inspiring novels (Peter Carey's *My Life As a Fake*), an Ern Malley Jazz Suite (by musician and former *Angry Penguins* contributor Dave Dallwitz), and a play about Malley, *The Black Swan of Trespass.*

"Princess, you lived in Princess St.,
   Where the urchins pick their nose in the sun
   With the left hand."

—FROM "PERSPECTIVE LOVESONG" BY ERN MALLEY

WAR OF THE WORDS

In the wee hours of one night/morning in 1956, New York DJ Jean Shepherd concocted a wild scheme to shake up the faith of "Day People" (in Shep's lingo, anyone who wasn't one of the "Night People" who listened to his 1–5:30 A.M. show) in the nation's supposedly authoritative best-seller lists. Shepherd solicited suggestions for elements of a fictional book from listeners, finally settling on *I, Libertine* by Frederick R. Ewing, a retired Commander in the Royal Navy and a scholar of 18th-century erotica (who, naturally, had never existed).

Armed with these details, Shepherd's listeners began requesting *I, Libertine* from every bookseller and library they knew—driving the nonexistent novel onto the best-seller lists and befuddling booksellers around the world. Yet one editor, Ian Ballantine, familiar with the source of the hoax, convinced Shepherd to team up with a real novelist to produce an actual book. The author they chose, curiously enough, was the sci-fi writer Theodore Sturgeon—a friend of Kurt Vonnegut and the inspiration for the fictional character Kilgore Trout (see pages 56 and 139–40) for *his* tangled tale). But Sturgeon was a notorious procrastinator and was eventually forced to bang out the complete manuscript in one marathon setting at Ballantine's home…only to fall asleep near the end, leaving Ballantine's wife to write the final chapter.

A TRUTH UNIVERSALLY REJECTED

David Lassman, the director of the Jane Austen Festival in Bath, England, was frustrated: He had spent three and a half years writing a novel but couldn't find a single publisher willing to buy it. Convinced that present-day publishers wouldn't recognize a great book if it bit them on the nose, he made slight changes to names and places in Austen's *Northanger Abbey* (substituting Austen's original title, *Susan*) and shipped sample chapters to 18 publishing houses in 2007. Some publishers returned the manuscript unread, refusing to read any work that didn't come from an agent; but those who did read his submission didn't detect the ruse, usually writing back to say the book was "not suitable for their lists." Acknowledging that *Northanger* wasn't one of Austen's best-known works, Lassman tried again with *Persuasion,* with nearly identical results. Finally, he shipped out the opening chapters of *Pride and Prejudice* (renamed *First Impressions*), complete with its instantly recognizable opening lines. "We don't feel that strongly about your work," responded one literary agent; another publisher said the book seemed "like a really original and interesting read," but didn't request additional chapters. Only one editor correctly identified the hoax, writing back that his own "first impressions" were "disbelief and mild annoyance—along, of course, with a moment's laughter."

....

" 'Gadzooks!' quoth I, 'but here's a saucy bawd!' "

—**"FREDERICK R. EWING,"** *I, LIBERTINE*

....

IF YOU DON'T KNOW ME BY NOW...

These writers found fame by compulsively chronicling the truth of their own sordid, hilarious, or shocking lives.

ME TALK TRUTHFULLY ONE DAY

One of America's funniest contemporary memoirists, David Sedaris has written about such events as disparate as taking guitar lessons (at age 12) from a midget named Mr. Mancini; being mistaken for a French pickpocket on the Paris Metro; and testing a kind of external catheter called a "Stadium Pal." A supposed "takedown" of Sedaris in 2007 compared his recollections with those of some of the real people mentioned in them and concluded that many facts had been highly exaggerated, if not completely made up. But Sedaris responded mainly with a shrug, noting that one *Esquire* assignment gave him "a whole new appreciation for people who can honestly tell the truth, because people didn't always say what I wanted them to." Still, in the wake of James Frey and other scandals, Sedaris bowed (slightly) to prevailing trends and added an author's note to his most recent book, describing its contents as "realish."

"When I am writing, I am there. I'm there . . . It's like a movie. It's extremely vivid. I'm a monkey at a typewriter, writing about the time it got M&Ms and the time a blue M&M came out instead of a red one."

—AUGUSTEN BURROUGHS

THE GREAT DEPRESSION

There seems to be an unwritten rule that the titles of raw, honest memoirs of depression must allude to classical works of art or literature—a rule that certainly holds true for these three authors.

Title	Origin of Title
William Styron, *Darkness Visible: A Memoir of Madness,* a chronicle of the *Sophie's Choice* author's bout with near-suicidal depression at age 60	Description of Hell, from Milton's *Paradise Lost:* *A dungeon horrible, on all sides round, As one great furnace flamed; yet from those flames No light, but rather darkness visible Served only to discover sights of woe*
Susanna Kaysen, *Girl, Interrupted,* a memoir of Kaysen's two-year stint in a mental hospital for treatment of borderline personality disorder	From the title of Jan Vermeer's painting *Girl Interrupted at her Music*—a figure she related to because her own life had been "interrupted in the music of being seventeen...one moment made to stand still and to stand for all the other moments, whatever they would be or might have been."
Rick Moody, *The Black Veil,* a meditation on Moody's struggles with addiction, paranoia, and psychiatric treatment	Nathaniel Hawthorne's story "The Minister's Black Veil," inspired by one Joseph Moody, who veiled himself after accidentally killing a childhood friend, and who was said to be an ancestor of Rick's (a family tale that turned out to be false).

THOSE MCCOURT BOYS

Though the McCourt brothers, Frank *(Angela's Ashes)* and Malachy *(A Monk Swimming)* have more or less established a monopoly on memoirs of hard-knock, Irish-American child-hoods, there are still stories left to tell—especially for younger brother Malachy. Some of the stranger pursuits of his adult life include a recurring Christmas role on *All My Children* as "Father Clarence"; a rather bleaker turn as the incarcerated Father Meehan on the HBO series *Oz;* and a run as Green Party candidate for governor of New York in 2006—a race he lost to Democrat Eliot Spitzer, who turned out to have a few sins of his own to confess.

AN HONEST MISTAKE

You would be forgiven for wondering if there are any Oprah-endorsed memoirists whose works *haven't* been debunked. Fortunately, there are people like Mitch Albom, whose best-selling *Tuesdays with Morrie*—a record of his conversations with a former professor who fought and died of Lou Gehrig's disease—has been inspiring readers for more than a decade. Yet Albom isn't entirely scandal free: In 2005 he was suspended, along with four other editors of the *Detroit Free Press,* over an Albom-penned column that incorrectly placed two NBA players in attendance at an NCAA game. Scrutiny of his complete publishing record failed to turn up evidence of a pattern of wrongdoing, and Albom's excuse turned out to be little more than an excess of trust: The players said they would attend, and he took them at their word.

WHAT IS THE WHAT'S FOR SALE?

Dave Eggers, author of the best-selling, Pulitzer Prize–nominated memoir *A Heartbreaking Work of Staggering Genius* (as well as *What Is the What,* a "fictionalized autobiography" of Sudanese refugee Valentino Achak Deng), is also the founder of 826 Valencia, a nonprofit group that operates writing and tutoring centers for students aged 8 to 18 in several major cities. The twist is that each center is "fronted" by a uniquely outlandish business that sells real—though not always functional—products that help to fund each location:

The Pirate Supply Store (826 Valencia, San Francisco, CA): "Scurvy Begone," sea sickness tablets, mermaid bait (and repellent)

Brooklyn Superhero Supply Co. (826NYC, Brooklyn, NY): Grappling hooks, superhero tights, antimatter

Echo Park Time Travel Mart (826LA, Echo Park, CA): Line of fragrances, including "Caveman," "Gold Rush," and "2012"

Greenwood Space Travel Supply Co. (826 Seattle, Seattle, WA): Space vehicle repair supplies, "Zero-Gravity Spaghetti Containment Device"

The Boring Store (826CHI, Chicago, IL): Secret-camera glasses, mustache disguise kits, heated stakeout gloves

Liberty Street Robot Supply & Repair (826michigan, Ann Arbor, MI): Positronic brains, robot first-aid kits, Robodentures

Greater Boston Bigfoot Research Institute (826 Boston, Roxbury, MA): Cryptozoology career kits, unicorn tears

DEAR DIARY

A survey of notable (and notorious) diaries from famous novelists, scientists, celebrities, and other famous scribblers.

....

> "My former boyfriend read [my diary] once, and he was mainly mad because he wasn't in it. I said, 'Yes, you are.' Then I looked, and he wasn't mentioned. It was as if he didn't exist. If you read somebody's diary, you get what you deserve."
> — **DAVID SEDARIS**

....

Lewis Carroll The *Alice in Wonderland* author's diaries filled at least 13 volumes, from 1855 through 1897, but only 9 volumes survive, and some are missing pages—including one page that apparently described the mysterious event that caused a rift between Carroll and the Liddell family, whose daughter Alice was the inspiration for Carroll's best-known book.

John Cheever Left behind a massive collection of journals— roughly 4,300 pages, most of them typed and single-spaced.

....

> "I am one of those old men; I am like a voyager who cannot remember the streams he has travelled."
> — **JOHN CHEEVER**

....

Anne Frank Received her first diary on her 13th birthday (June 12, 1942) and addressed it about its place among her gifts, "The first to greet me was you, possibly the nicest of all." She kept writing for more than two years, pausing in May 1944 to recopy earlier entries. Her complete diary totaled 324 handwritten pages—which have been translated into at least 67 languages.

"I keep my ideals, because in spite of everything I still believe that people are really good at heart."

—ANNE FRANK

Kurt Cobain The Nirvana frontman filled 23 notebooks, amounting to some 800 pages, with everything from early drafts of hits like "Smells Like Teen Spirit" to his favorite CDs, unsent letters, and lists of rules for the band.

"There are a lot of bands who claim to be alternative and theyre [sic] nothing but stripped down, ex sunset strip hair farming bands of a few years ago. I would love to be erased from our association with Pearl Jam or the Nymphs and other first time offenders."

—KURT COBAIN

Charles Darwin The origin of the great naturalist's own *On the Origin of Species* lay within the diaries he kept on board the HMS *Beagle* as it traveled around the world. His total output included: at least 18 volumes of rough field notes; a four-volume zoological diary; a three-volume geological diary; an extensive catalogue of specimens; and an 800-page personal diary of the five-year journey.

Anna Dostoyevsky The second wife of the great novelist—they met when she was hired to transcribe his dictated text of *The Gambler*—read her famous husband's mail but kept her own diary secret from him by using a private shorthand, the code for which wasn't fully cracked until years after her death.

Buckminster Fuller The renowned author, architect, and inventor is responsible for one of the most impressive diaries in human history. Known as the "Dymaxion Chronofile," the diary contains a complete chronicle of his life from 1915 to 1983, including daily activities, newspaper clippings, receipts, and correspondence . . . adding up to roughly 270 linear feet of paper.

....

"I could not be judge of what was valid to put in or not. I must put everything in, so I started a very rigorous record."

—BUCKMINSTER FULLER

....

Johanna Fantova Don't recognize the name? Fantova was Albert Einstein's last girlfriend, and her 62-page diary is the only known journal kept by a personal friend of Einstein at the end of his life. It includes poems he wrote to her and a wealth of surprising facts: For example, after deciding that a parrot received on his 75th birthday was "depressed," Einstein tried to cheer it up by telling bad jokes.

....

"[Einstein] tried all day to compose a radio message on behalf of Israel and did not succeed in finishing it. He claims he is totally stupid—that he has always thought so, and that only once in a while was he able to accomplish something."

—Johanna Fantova

....

THE AMERICAN WAY

Although an official "Presidential Daily Diary" exists for most presidents since Washington, it's only a rough chronicle of daily movements, meetings, and conversations, jotted down by secretaries. Through the end of the 19th century, only four presidents had kept personal diaries for large portions of their adult lives: George Washington, John Quincy Adams, James K. Polk, and Rutherford B. Hayes. And of those, only Adams's extraordinarily detailed journals (covering some 68 years) offer much entertainment or candid insight into the man. A gap of

100 years stands between Hayes and the next dutiful presidential diarist: Ronald Reagan. The Gipper, who self-censored curse words, wrote in his diary every day except while hospitalized after an assassination attempt. Upon resuming his diary, he noted: "Getting shot hurts."

....

"Wrote nothing."

—FRANZ KAFKA, JUNE 1, 1912, DIARY ENTRY

....

BLOGGING THE BLACK PLAGUE

Samuel Pepys (1633–1703) was born the son of a London tailor, attended Cambridge University's Magdalene College, and for most of his adult life rose steadily through the ranks of government service: He later served as Secretary to the Admiralty, a member of Parliament, and President of the Royal Society, and he helped lay the groundwork for England's first professional naval service. But his greatest legacy is the diary he kept from 1660–69—from age 27 to age 36, when he quit from fear of going blind—which is now regarded as one of England's national treasures and one of the most important diaries in history. As luck (of sorts) would have it, Pepys lived through two of the greatest disasters in English history: the Plague (1665–66) and the Great Fire of London (1666), both of which he chronicled in great and humanizing detail, along with scenes from his public life, commentary on cultural happenings (such as attending *The Woman's Prize, or the Tamer Tamed,* John Fletcher's sequel to *The Taming of the Shrew*), and his not-infrequent attempts to seduce random women around town.

PEN PALS

Romantic or grouchy, supportive or snarky, these well-known authors were also legendary letter writers.

Jane Austen is said to have been a prolific letter writer, though only about 160 letters (of an estimated 3,000) have survived: Most of the others were destroyed by recipients, many of whom were family members looking to protect Jane's privacy. A large number of the remaining letters were addressed to Austen's niece, Fanny Knight, advising the girl on her love life and conveying characteristic wit. Commenting about one of Fanny's acquaintances, who disapproved of Austen's writing, Jane wrote that "he deserves better treatment than to be obliged to read any more of my works."

Mark Twain, oddly enough, took the time in at least two personal letters to vent his loathing for Austen's prose. In 1898, he commented: "Every time I read 'Pride and Prejudice' I want to dig her up and beat her over the skull with her own shin-bone." And in a 1909 letter, criticizing another author's work, he wrote: "To me his prose is unreadable—like Jane Austin's [sic]. No there is a difference. I could read his prose on salary, but not Jane's. Jane is entirely impossible. It seems a great pity that they allowed her to die a natural death."

Ezra Pound and James Joyce carried on a decades-long personal correspondence, much of it revolving around Pound's efforts to place Joyce's stories in various magazines and to champion his longer works against harsh criticism (even *Finnegan's Wake,* which Pound once described as "toilet humor"). When one batch of stories was turned down by the magazine *The Smart Set,* Pound passed along the rejection note with a cover letter that began, "Dear Joyce: I enclose a prize sample of bull shit."

H. P. Lovecraft spent the latter years of his life living in Providence, Rhode Island, keeping in touch with friends and business acquaintances primarily through the mail. The already-prolific Lovecraft is said to have written an estimated 100,000 letters in his lifetime, of which 20,000 survive. For years, he wrote an estimated 40,000 words annually to fellow horror writer Clark Ashton Smith—often commenting on the petty frustrations of the writer's existence. Smoldering from one recent rejection by the Knopf publishing house, he wrote to Smith that "Knopf should remove the Borzoi from his imprint, and substitute either the Golden Calf or a jackass with brazen posteriors."

Elizabeth Barrett and Robert Browning: In 1845 the eminent poets began one of the most famous correspondences of all time, exchanging 574 letters over 20 months as their love for each other blossomed. Barrett's father forbade her from pursuing a relationship with Browning, so the star-crossed lovers eloped to Italy. Barrett sought reconciliation after her father disinherited her—only to discover years later that her father never even opened the many letters she had sent.

BOOKS THAT CHANGED THE WORLD

PLATO,
THE REPUBLIC (380 B.C.)

Why it's important: *The Republic* has had an enormous influence on philosophical and political thought, from ancient times to today. The Socratic dialogue is chiefly concerned with the concept of justice—specifically, whether the just man is happier than the unjust—but also touches on poetry, philosophy, and the immortality of the soul. The famous "Allegory of the Cave"—which attempts to illustrate that ideas, and not the things we perceive, are the "true" reality—comes from this work.

What you don't know: If you don't like poetry, you might find a kindred spirit in Plato: He (or rather, Socrates) proclaims near the end of the book that all poets will be banished from his ideal society because they produce "phantoms, not realities." *The Republic* also introduces the allegory of the Ring of Gyges, in which a shepherd discovers a magic ring that grants invisibility. The story—an acknowledged source for the "One Ring" of Tolkien's *The Lord of the Rings*—is part of an argument over whether all people would be unjust . . . if they could only get away with it.

THOMAS PAINE,
COMMON SENSE (1776)

Why it's important: Paine's pamphlet (originally titled "Plain Truth") was the first published work to call for the independence of the American colonies.

What you don't know: Paine was a rabble-rouser before he ever came to America—a tendency that was noted by Benjamin Franklin, who sponsored Paine's emigration. But like Franklin, Paine's talents extended into many other spheres: When he wasn't publishing incendiary political tracts, he even worked as an inventor, creating a new kind of iron bridge and a smokeless candle. His work was a strong influence on and inspiration to a young Thomas Edison, who later wrote that Paine "had a sort of universal genius."

....

"Society in every state is a blessing, but government even in its best state is but a necessary evil; in its worst state an intolerable one; for when we suffer, or are exposed to the same miseries BY A GOVERNMENT, which we might expect in a country WITHOUT GOVERNMENT, our calamity is heightened by reflecting that we furnish the means by which we suffer."

—Thomas Paine, *Common Sense*

....

ADAM SMITH, *THE WEALTH OF NATIONS* (1776)

Why it's important: Smith's tome provides a rationale for a global transformation from mercantilism—the primary economic theory from the 16th through the 18th centuries—to capitalism. Whenever you hear about a "laissez-faire" economic doctrine (Smith didn't introduce the doctrine, but this volume was its biggest proponent) or the "invisible hand" of the market, you're hearing the words of Adam Smith.

What you don't know: Book V contains a critique of English universities, which Smith believed to be inferior to their Scottish counterparts. Fortunately, it took the English only a couple of centuries to get over this slander: In March 2007, Smith became the first Scotsman to be featured on an English banknote.

MARY WOLLSTONECRAFT, *A VINDICATION OF THE RIGHTS OF WOMAN* (1792)

Why it's important: Wollstonecraft argued that women were as capable of rational thought as men, lacking only the benefit of formal education to develop their natural abilities. Many of her ideas wouldn't quite qualify as modern feminist thought, but they were certainly ahead of her time.

What you don't know: If anything, her personal life was actually more modern than her writing: Wollstonecraft had a long (and long-distance) romantic relationship with author William Godwin, but both were opposed to marriage as an institution that promoted inequality of the sexes. When Wollstonecraft became pregnant—with a daughter, also named Mary, who would go on to write *Frankenstein*—the two married for the sake of the child, but Wollstonecraft died in childbirth.

ALEXIS DE TOCQUEVILLE,
DEMOCRACY IN AMERICA (1835)

Why it's important: Tocqueville's book attempted to show why the American system of government had succeeded, when similar systems had failed in so many other places. It remains an insightful, readable, and oft-quoted analysis of contemporary politics and of dangers that could (and did) arise to challenge democracy in the United States.

What you don't know: This is *not* the book Tocqueville (age 25) and his partner, Gustave de Beaumont (28), were commissioned to write. France's King Louis-Phillipe had sent them to America to write an analysis of the nation's prison system. Incredibly, they managed to deliver on that promise, too: *The U.S. Penitentiary System and Its Application in France,* which drew on interviews with prison officials and prisoners across the country, contributed to the reform of the prison system in France.

KARL MARX AND FRIEDRICH ENGELS,
THE COMMUNIST MANIFESTO (1848)

Why it's important: This brief (only 23 pages, in its first appearance) declaration of principles inspired the major communist political systems of the 20th century—and thus was partially responsible for the cold war.

What you don't know: Though Karl Marx (and his magnificent beard) loom large in any modern discussion of communism, the *Manifesto* was first published without authorial attribution. Marx was a 30-year-old historian and political philosopher who was well known in radical socialist circles but was far from a household name. Soon after moving to London in 1847, he began meeting with a coalition of working-class parties who dubbed themselves "The Communist League" and who commissioned Marx to write down a statement of their principles. The manifesto was published anonymously in 1848; the first edition bearing Marx's name didn't appear until 1850, in an English-language printing.

THE BEARD TO BEAT

In 2008 the London *Times* dubbed Karl Marx's facial hair the #1 beard of all time—beating out even Charles Dickens (#5), Soviet leader Vladimir Lenin (#6), and ZZ Top's Billy Gibbons and Dusty Hill (#10).

HARRIET BEECHER STOWE,
UNCLE TOM'S CABIN (1852)

Why it's important: Stowe's novel, first serialized in 40 installments in the antislavery periodical *The National Era* (for a fee of $300), put a human face on the issue of slavery. Her book won thousands of new converts to the abolitionist cause, allegedly inspiring President Abraham Lincoln to remark, upon meeting Stowe in 1862, "So you're the little woman who wrote the book that made this great war!" *Uncle Tom's Cabin* stands as perhaps the first "muckraking novel" in America (though that term wasn't coined until 1906, in a speech by President Roosevelt), and it directly inspired later activist writers, including Upton Sinclair and Rachel Carson.

What you don't know: Stowe's novel wasn't only an influential book, it was a bona fide blockbuster best seller. *Uncle Tom's Cabin* reportedly sold 3,000 copies in its first day, 10,000 in one week, and 300,000 in its first year—at a time when the total U.S. population was just over 23 million. In 1853, *Putnam's Monthly* magazine said that "all other successes in literature were failures when compared with the success of *Uncle Tom*."

A NOT-SO-CIVIL BUSINESS

In an ironic twist of fate, J. P. Jewett, Stowe's first publisher, was driven out of business by the Civil War. Jewett moved on to less history-making pursuits, including selling "Peruvian Syrup" (a medicinal "iron tonic") and working as a patent agent.

CHARLES DARWIN,
ON THE ORIGIN OF SPECIES (1859)

Why it's important: Darwin's revolutionary work (published 23 years after his five-year voyage on the HMS *Beagle*) introduced the concept of natural selection as the driving force in the development and diversification of species, upending centuries of erroneous thought about how and why various species came into being. Although it would be nearly 100 years before the discovery of DNA's double helix, his theories still form the foundation of virtually all modern biological science.

What you don't know: For some people, Darwin's name has come to symbolize a coldly scientific (if not atheistic) view of existence. But he was by all accounts a funny, kind, and gentle family man, who was profoundly awed by nature and felt a deep compassion for his fellow man. In fact, though he lived in a time when slavery was common, Darwin himself was a staunch abolitionist: he once said that "It makes one's blood boil, yet heart tremble, to think that we Englishmen and our American descendants, with their boastful cry of liberty, have been and are so guilty."

A TANGLED FAMILY TREE

Darwin's expert understanding of the inheritance of traits within species made him extra-anxious about his own breeding—or rather, inbreeding: he married his first cousin. But despite his concerns, all of his children who survived childhood were perfectly healthy, if not outright exceptional: among his five sons were a banker, an army officer, an astronomer, a botanist, and an engineer. (There is some speculation, however, that his sixth son, who died at 18 months old, was born with Down syndrome.)

UPTON SINCLAIR, *THE JUNGLE* (1906)

Why it's important: Sinclair's novel was filled with graphic detail about American slaughterhouses: poisoned rats ground up in sausage machines, diseased and spoiled beef sold to consumers, and workers using factory floors as toilets. The book sparked immediate worldwide outrage—purchases of American meat dropped by 50 percent at home and abroad—and led Congress to pass both the Meat Inspection Act and the Pure Food and Drug Act within only six months.

What you don't know: Sinclair, a fervent supporter of the Socialist party, wasn't primarily concerned with the health of the American consumer: He wrote the book hoping to win support for the factory workers who toiled under intolerable conditions. Slaughterhouse workers labored 12-hour days, were often ripped off by their employers, and were regularly maimed, burned, and blinded in the line of work—but the public was more shocked by the handful of pages describing dead rats and rotting meat. As Sinclair cleverly put it, "I aimed at the public's heart, and by accident I hit it in the stomach."

Although *The Jungle* failed to spark a Socialist revolution on its own, Sinclair used his profits from the book to build a utopian colony named "Helicon Hall" on the site of a boys' school (complete with swimming pool and bowling alley) near Englewood, New Jersey. But even this stab at promoting Socialist ideals fell short: Helicon Hall burned down after 4 months.

STARTING AT THE BOTTOM

Sinclair Lewis, 1930 Nobel Prize winner, worked as a janitor for 2 months at Helicon Hall.

JANE JACOBS,
THE DEATH AND LIFE OF GREAT AMERICAN CITIES (1961)

Why it's important: Jacobs contradicted the contemporary wisdom of modernist urban planners such as Robert Moses and Le Corbusier, who advocated efficient, segmented use of limited urban space, rather than Jacobs's ideal of neighborhoods of mixed-use blocks.

What you don't know: Jane Jacobs's theories were far from theoretical: she is well-remembered in New York's Greenwich Village for leading the fight against a Robert Moses–envisioned superhighway that threatened to cut a bisecting swath through lower Manhattan. She achieved similar success in Toronto, Ontario, where she joined the successful fight against the Spadina Expressway. Known as somewhat eccentric, Jacobs admitted to making many of her arguments in imaginary conversations with Thomas Jefferson—who, when she ran out of things to tell him, she replaced with Benjamin Franklin: "Like Jefferson, he was interested in lofty things, but also in nitty-gritty, down-to-earth details, such as why the alley we were walking through wasn't paved, and who would pave it if it were paved. He was interested in everything, so he was a very satisfying companion."

RACHEL CARSON,
SILENT SPRING (1962)

Why it's important: With its vivid description of a typical American town "silenced" from the devastating effects of the pesticide DDT boomeranging throughout the food chain, *Silent Spring* directly led to a ban on DDT, increased government oversight of pesticide and other chemical manufacturing industries, and heightened public awareness of mankind's ability to damage the environment.

What you don't know: This now-classic book was a harder sell than many people realize. DDT was invented in 1939 and was used heavily in World War II to purge South Pacific islands of malaria-carrying insects. In 1945, the pesticide passed into widespread civilian use; Carson tried to interest U.S. magazines (including *Reader's Digest*) in a story about the unexplored long-term effects of DDT but was shot down. Thirteen years later, a friend alerted Carson to large-scale bird deaths resulting from DDT use, but again Carson failed to secure interest from magazine publishers—even though she had become a best-selling author with a trilogy of books about ocean life: *The Sea Around Us* (1951), *The Edge of the Sea* (1955), and *Under the Sea Wind* (1941). It took another four years for Carson to write the book—and eight more years before the Environmental Protection Agency came into being, under President Richard Nixon (1970).

RALPH NADER, *UNSAFE AT ANY SPEED* (1965)

Why it's important: Nader's groundbreaking exposé of unsafe American automotive products led directly to the 1966 National Traffic and Motor Vehicle Safety Act, ensuring that all vehicles sold in the United States meet certain basic safety standards.

What you don't know: Nader first formulated the central argument of the book as a Harvard Law student, in an article entitled "American Cars: Designed for Death." When the book was finally published, General Motors hired a private detective to follow Nader and dig up information to discredit him, but Nader sued GM for invasion of privacy and eventually won $280,000 from the chastened automaker. Nader funneled much of that settlement into efforts to overhaul other industries, including meat processing and insecticide regulation; no doubt, Sinclair and Carson would have approved.

SIMPLY THE WORST

Unsafe at Any Speed singled out GM's Corvair for particular scorn (the car also made *Time* magazine's list of the 50 Worst Cars of All Time). The rear-engine layout made it hard to handle; fumes from the heating system seeped into the cabin; some models had a gasoline-burning heater in the front trunk; and in the event of a head-on collision, the driver risked impalement on the single-piece steering column. The impalement-averse American public stopped buying the Corvair in droves, sending sales plummeting from 220,000 in 1965 to 14,800 in 1968.

OFF THE PAGE

Sometimes, the most intriguing stories can't be found under
the covers *or* between the sheets. How did famous authors
choose their pseudonyms...and why did some of them have no
choice? Which big-time best-selling authors have been known
to rock out almost as much as they write down? And how many
writers experienced family and relationship drama that rivaled
anything they set down on the page?

IMAGINARY FRIENDS

What happens when fictional characters suddenly start publishing books of their own—or when real people transform into cartoons? Here are a handful of mind-bending instances where the lines between fiction and reality were more than blurred.

SOMETHING'S FISHY

One of Kurt Vonnegut's most-loved characters (or at least most-used, appearing in person in three novels and named in three others), ever-struggling sci-fi writer Kilgore Trout, boasts one of the stranger biographies of any fictional creation. Trout was based on the real-life science-fiction writer Theodore Sturgeon, a friend of Vonnegut's who—like Trout—had failed to attract an audience beyond die-hard genre fans. Fans of Vonnegut's *Breakfast of Champions* will recall that Trout and Vonnegut actually meet near the end of the book—but even Vonnegut couldn't have imagined that his fictional character would break into the real world at a later date.

Yet another sometime sci-fi author, Philip José Farmer, while suffering from writer's block, decided to try his hand at writing a Kilgore Trout novel—and ultimately published *Venus on the Half-Shell* (1975) under Trout's name, with no hint of its true authorship. Farmer appears in an author photo virtually buried in a fake beard. The book went through dozens of printings, mostly because of the Vonnegut connection, but Vonnegut was not amused and refused to allow any more Trout books to be published. Farmer claimed that the book was meant to be nothing more than a tribute to one of his favorite writers and characters. And perhaps fittingly, he also maintained that he had profited less from this title than from many of his own titles, citing rumors that his publisher had siphoned off most of his royalties—a situation that would have been familiar to the fictional Trout.

KILGORE'S BELIEVE IT OR NOT

Though "Theodore Sturgeon" seems as if it couldn't be anything other than a pseudonym, and Sturgeon was born "Edward Hamilton Waldo," the former really was his legal name. After his father walked out, his mother married a man named William Sturgeon; young Edward adopted his new father's last name and changed his first from Edward (his birth father's name) to Theodore to better match his childhood nickname, "Teddy." Simple, right?

AN ANIMATED EXISTENCE

The real-life antics of legendary "gonzo" journalist Hunter S. Thompson seem almost cartoonishly bizarre at times; maybe that's why the man has been such a rich source of inspiration for cartoon and comic book characters:

Uncle Duke: a recurring character in Garry Trudeau's *Doonesbury* strip, whose omnipresent cigarette holder and fondness for recreational drug use (see pages 24–29) mark him as an obvious homage to Thompson—who once said, "I've never met Garry Trudeau, but if I ever do, I'll set him on fire."

Spider Jerusalem: the crusading gonzo journalist of the future from Warren Ellis's *Transmetropolitan* comic book series. The real Thompson was an aficionado of large firearms; Jerusalem shares this affinity, though his weapon of choice is the "bowel disruptor." Need we say more?

Hunter Gathers: a military officer on the Cartoon Network's animated television show *Venture Bros.* Given his response to Trudeau's Uncle Duke (and his fondness for big guns), one shudders to think what the late Thompson would have threatened to do to the creators of the transsexual Gathers.

HARRY POTTER AND THE MAGICAL MYSTERY BIDDER

Though Harry Potter's epic saga has come to an end, several "real" books from his fictional world have magically appeared in our own: Newt Scamander's *Fantastic Beasts and Where to Find Them,* Kennilworthy Whisp's *Quidditch Through the Ages,* and *The Tales of Beedle the Bard.* They were really written, of course, by *Harry Potter* author J. K. Rowling, who created them to raise money for charity. An original, handwritten copy of *Beedle* even made history in 2007 when it was purchased at an auction by a mystery bidder, later revealed to be online retailer Amazon, for nearly 2 million British pounds ($3.97 million)—the highest price ever paid at auction for a modern literary manuscript.

DON'T ASK, DO TELL

Of all the untold stories in the Harry Potter universe, it's doubtful that any will cause as much commotion as J. K. Rowling's 2007 revelation, in front of a packed house at Carnegie Hall, that in her mind Hogwarts headmaster Albus Dumbledore was gay. When the audience erupted in several minutes of sustained applause, a stunned Rowling added, "I would have told you earlier if I knew it would make you so happy."

A.K.A.

Here's the straight story behind a few authors who changed their identities—some out of necessity, some just for fun, and some practically by accident.

BIG NAMES

Lewis Carroll (Charles Lutwidge Dodgson): Chosen, in typically brain-teasing style, by translating his first two names into Latin (Carolus Lodovicus) and then anglicizing them.

George Orwell (Eric Blair): Would we still be studying *1984*'s Newspeak if it had been written by H. Lewis Allways? That was one of four pseudonyms a 29-year-old Eric Blair suggested to his editor, along with Kenneth Miles, P. S. Burton, and the eventual winner—borrowed from the River Orwell in Suffolk, England.

Dav Pilkey (Dave Pilkey): OK, so it's not much of a pseudonym; when a teenaged Dave worked at Pizza Hut, a broken label-maker spat out "Dav" instead of "Dave" for his nametag, and Pilkey stuck with it.

Lemony Snicket (Daniel Handler): Handler used the name Lemony Snicket as a joke when he was researching right-wing organizations for his first (non-Lemony) novel *The Basic Eight*; when he started writing children's books, he kept it and also gave his narrator the well-worn pseudonym.

Henry David Thoreau (David Henry Thoreau): What can be said about this, except that it may be the least interesting pseudonym of all time?

ALTER EGOS

Ray Bradbury: At times, this remarkably prolific writer was even more prolific than many people knew, thanks to his frequent use of pseudonyms. At age 19, he began publishing a short fanzine with a group of friends. The first issue contained an editorial and poem by Bradbury and a story by Ron Reynolds—a Bradbury pseudonym, created to give the illusion that more people had contributed to the magazine. The second issue contained no less than three Bradbury pseudonyms—a short story by Anthony Corvais, an article by Guy Amory, and a poem by Doug Rogers (a combination of Bradbury's middle name and Buck Rogers). Even Bradbury's breakthrough into "quality" fiction occurred under a pseudonym: In 1945 he had three stories accepted almost simultaneously by prestigious publications (*Mademoiselle, Charm,* and *Collier's*) under the name William Elliott—which prompted some quick phone calls to editors to prevent uncashable checks from being sent out to the nonexistent authors.

Anne, Charlotte, and Emily Brontë: The Brontë sisters lived in a time when female authors would commonly publish their works under a male pseudonym to avoid prejudice against works by women, and the Brontës were no exception.

A ROSE BY ANY OTHER NAME

The prejudice against women writers, sad to say, hasn't been entirely erased: Even J. K. Rowling is a pen name—chosen because Joanne Rowling's publisher believed that young boys were less likely to buy books that were obviously written by women.

They assumed the identities of three rather androgynously named brothers rather than take distinct pseudonymous surnames; thus, the world was introduced to Acton, Currer, and Ellis Bell. But even false identities weren't a guarantee of success: The now-renowned writers' first book, a self-published collection of poems by all three sisters, sold a none-too-promising two copies—though one reviewer noted some promise in "Ellis's" work.

Stephen King: Early in his career, the prolific King was told by his publishers that the public "wouldn't accept" more than one new book a year from a writer, so he began mixing in books written under a pseudonym with his regular publications. The first book to appear under a pseudonym was *Rage* (1977); King originally planned to publish it under his maternal grandfather's name (Gus Pillsbury), but because word had gotten out about the fake name, he had to make a last-minute change. When the publisher called to ask for a final pseudonym, King looked around his desk: He saw a novel by Richard Stark and heard Bachman Turner Overdrive playing on the stereo... thus, "Richard Bachman" was born. (The song, if you must know, was "You Ain't Seen Nothin' Yet.")

Gore Vidal: Though he eventually became one of the most respected figures in contemporary thought and literature, some of his early works—especially *The City and the Pillar* (1948)—outraged critics (and prompted some to boycott his novels) because of Vidal's frank and open treatment of homosexuality. Facing a blacklist, Vidal turned to genre fiction and produced three murder mysteries under the name Edgar Box: *Death in the Fifth Position, Death Before Bedtime,* and *Death Likes it Hot.* But these weren't Vidal's only forays into the world of pen names: He also wrote a book in the "international intrigue" genre, *Thieves Fall Out* (1953) by "Cameron Kay," and a Hollywood melodrama entitled *A Star's Progress* (1950) by "Katherine Everard"— whose last name was borrowed from a gay bathhouse in New York City.

Michael Chabon: When authors create literary alter egos for themselves, they usually don't go further than dreaming up a phony name. But for Michael Chabon, that wasn't far enough: August Van Zorn, "the greatest unknown horror writer of the twentieth century," was first mentioned in Chabon's *Wonder Boys* (1995), and was later credited as the author of a story called *The Black Mill* in Chabon's *Werewolves in Their Youth* (1999). But far from being a mere pseudonym, Chabon's alter ego boasted not only a detailed biography (his "real" name was Albert Vetch), but also a bibliography of more than 60 published works (including "Cock Robin," "The Pig God," and "The Rage of Elvira Ogletree"), and a short-story competition sponsored by *McSweeney's* magazine: The August Van Zorn Prize for the Weird Short Story. Chabon even invented a literary scholar—the anagrammatic "Leon Chaim Bach"—devoted solely to Van Zorn's works.

TIME TO MAKE
THE DOUGHNUTS

A writer's life is legendarily difficult, and all but the most successful authors have had to find other ways to pay the bills in between
royalty checks. Sometimes those money-making schemes have
been their downfall (Mark Twain, we're looking at you!); for
others, the moonlighting has been almost as noteworthy as their
books. And even the biggest best-selling authors sometimes dip
their toes into other careers. Who knew that the super-successful,
hyper-educated Amy Tan was secretly dying to become a whip-
cracking rock and roll dominatrix?

DOWN AND OUT

It's the oldest story in the book, so to speak: promising young
writer toils away in obscurity, living hand-to-mouth in a string
of dingy, degrading, and sometimes bizarre jobs, just waiting for
the royalty checks to start rolling in. Sometimes those lousy jobs
form the basis of great works of fiction...and sometimes they're
better left forgotten.

Maya Angelou: It's hard to imagine Bill Clinton's dignified in-
augural poet in such a position, but Maya Angelou worked
at various times as a fry cook, a nightclub "shake dancer,"
and even a prostitute manager—all during a period in her
late teens after she had given birth to her first son. But
it wasn't all grit and grime for the young Angelou; she
became the first black streetcar conductor in San Francisco before graduating from high school, and later went
on to dance with Alvin Ailey and to work closely with both

Martin Luther King Jr. and Malcolm X in the civil rights movement.

Jeffrey Eugenides: *Middlesex* author Jeffrey Eugenides volunteered briefly at Mother Teresa's hospice in Calcutta during a college break, but it seems the sainted nun's ethics didn't completely rub off on Eugenides. He later lost a job at the Academy of American Poets after being caught working on his first novel, *The Virgin Suicides*, during business hours.

David Mamet: It probably comes as little surprise to fans of David Mamet's tough, trash-talking drama that the author spent time working for the hard-core pornographic magazine *Oui*...not as an editor but as a caption writer. Oddly, Mamet recalls the job as being "too hard," because it took an activity he enjoyed (looking at pictures of naked women) and turned it into "homework."

Arthur Miller: Though he would later gain distinction as one of America's greatest dramatists, win the Pulitzer Prize, and marry Marilyn Monroe, Arthur Miller paid his dues in a variety of menial jobs—including a $15-per-month stint in a "mouse house," feeding mice used in medical experiments.

John Steinbeck: The classic chronicler of America's working class spent well-known stints working as a fruit picker (which provided material for *Of Mice and Men*) and as a reporter in San Francisco (generating articles that provided the foundation of *The Grapes of Wrath*). But Steinbeck also pulled a less fruitful stint in New York City in 1925, where he worked on the construction of Madison Square Garden.

John Kennedy Toole: Unlike his memorable antihero Ignatius Reilly (*A Confederacy of Dunces,* 1980), who claimed he had never gone farther from New Orleans than Baton Rouge, John Kennedy Toole saw a great deal of the outside world: He received a master's degree from Columbia University and spent two years teaching English to Army recruits in Puerto Rico. Back at home, Toole spent time working in a men's clothing factory and helped a friend sell food from a street cart—both episodes that showed up in his novel—and like the gruff Reilly, Toole lived out the latter part of his tragically short life with his domineering mother in New Orleans.

ROCK BOTTOM OR TOP OF THE HEAP?

In publishing lingo, a "remainder" is an author's worst nightmare: It's a book that a publisher has sold off at a deep discount (usually too deep to generate royalties for the author) to make room for new titles. But that isn't a big concern for the members of the Rock Bottom Remainders, an occasional rock and roll supergroup whose revolving member list has boasted some of the biggest names on contemporary best-seller lists, including Stephen King, Dave Barry, Mitch Albom, Scott Turow, and Amy Tan.

The Remainders were founded in 1992 by Kathi Kamen Goldmark, a musician who worked part-time driving authors on book tours. She found that many of them were more interested in talking about music than writing, and she eventually put together an ad hoc group of author-musicians to perform a benefit concert at a Los Angeles book fair. Founding member Dave Barry is fond of saying that the group "plays music as well as Metallica writes novels," though some members, including Albom and Ridley

Pearson, worked as professional musicians before their writing careers took off.

Despite the occasional presence of superstar guests like Warren Zevon and Bruce Springsteen, none of the regular members take things too seriously: Über-best-seller Scott Turow tends to take the stage wearing a huge curly blond wig, and *Joy Luck Club* author Amy Tan dons skin-tight leather and carries a whip to sing her signature tune, "These Boots Are Made for Walking."

> *"The book of my enemy has been remaindered*
> *And I am pleased."*
>
> —CLIVE JAMES

THE ROCK AND ROLLER'S GUIDE TO THE GALAXY

English author Douglas Adams (1951–2001) is best remembered as the man who dreamed up the *Hitchhiker's Guide to the Galaxy*, the wisecracking and seemingly infinite "standard repository for all knowledge and wisdom" in the humorous sci-fi book series of the same name. Fans may also remember numerous rock and roll references throughout the books, with a particular predilection for British bands like Dire Straits and The Beatles. But Adams was more than a mere fan; he was an accomplished amateur musician—and an occasional member of the Rock Bottom Remainders—who was friends with a number of bona fide rock stars, including Pink Floyd guitarist David Gilmour. The fictional rock band Disaster Area, whose apocalyptic stage show plays a pivotal role in Adams's *The Restaurant at the End of the Universe*, was inspired by Pink Floyd—and Gilmour returned the favor by inviting Adams to name the 1994 Pink Floyd album *The Division Bell* (a name that Adams simply chose from the album's lyrics).

MUSIC TO HIS EARS

Daniel Handler, aka Lemony Snicket, has had a rather fitting (and semi-thriving) side career as a musician: he plays accordion on several albums, including The Magnetic Fields's album *69 Love Songs,* and wrote the lyrics for One Ring Zero's song "Radio." But he hasn't let his musical success go to his head: "If you play the accordion," he has said, "you're usually the best accordion player anyone knows."

THE MOTHER (AND FATHERS) OF INVENTION

For some who live "the life of the mind," the drive to invent carries over into other creative areas. Writers of sci-fi or speculative fiction may be more susceptible than most, but the bug can strike virtually anyone.

Margaret Atwood: Margaret Atwood made her reputation with speculative fiction like *The Handmaid's Tale* but also had a hand—so to speak—in the development of a gizmo that could have come straight out of science fiction. Weary of long author tours, Atwood dreamed up the LongPen, a "remote signing device" that allows authors to sit comfortably at home, communicating with fans at book signing events via webcam and signing books with an Internet-linked mechanical arm. Unotchit Inc., makers of the device, claim that it has prevented 76 tons of carbon dioxide emissions; no word yet on how they'll tackle robot writer's cramp.

Roald Dahl: In real life, Roald Dahl didn't quite match the inventive output of his manic chocolate-wizard Willy Wonka—but he did play a role in the creation of a device arguably more important than the Everlasting Gobstopper. Dahl's son was struck by a car in 1960 and suffered from excess fluid buildup in his brain. The best available shunt (a valve to drain excess fluid) was prone to blockage, so Dahl, a model aircraft enthusiast, worked with fellow flyer Stanley Wade—who specialized in tiny hydraulics—and neurosurgeon Kenneth Till to develop an improved model. The Wade-Dahl-Till (WDT) valve spared Dahl's son and thousands of other patients from complications of hydrocephaly, and the Roald Dahl Foundation continues to provide funds for young people suffering from neurological conditions.

Neal Stephenson: Notoriously erudite and verbose (his *Baroque Trilogy* runs to some 2,600 pages), Neal Stephenson's fascination with advanced technology has led him to pursue some impressively complex schemes in service of his books—from programming software to generate maps for his book *Cryptomonicon* to inventing a new language in *Anathem*. He also spent several years working for Blue Origin, the private aerospace company that was started by Amazon.com founder Jeff Bezos, studying different kinds of space launch technologies. Stephenson even lent a hand in the construction of *Blue Origin Goddard*, a prototype space vehicle test flown in November 2006.

THE STEPFATHER OF INVENTION?

Samuel Langhorne Clemens reinvented himself as Mark Twain and created dozens of unforgettable characters like Tom Sawyer and Huck Finn. He was also friends with Nikola Tesla and fancied himself something of an inventor in other fields—but his track record off the page wasn't so stellar. Twain created just one profitable product, a scrapbook with preglued pages that made him some $12,000 in profits over a short period. Other personal projects, including a clamp designed to keep infants from kicking off their bedsheets, were disappointing failures, and Twain proved even less astute at evaluating other people's inventions. Among his notable investment failures were:

Invention	Twain Invested	The Result
Kaolatype (method of printing illustrations)	$50,000	Never took off; supplanted by other printing technology
Paige Compositor (an automated typesetting machine)	$300,000	Drained Twain's fortune and most of his wife's inheritance
Method of carrying human voice by electric wire	$0	In a rare moment of restraint, Twain refused to invest in the one product that could have made him ridiculously wealthy: Alexander Graham Bell's telephone

WUNDERKIND

Most authors pay the bills during their early attempts at writing with not-so-desirable jobs—but not James Patterson, who was conspicuously successful long before he launched into true literary superstardom. For years, Patterson had flirted on and off with writing, even winning an Edgar Award for best first novel in 1977. But while serving as youngest-ever CEO of the J. Walter Thompson ad agency—where he created the memorable "Toys R Us Kid" campaign—Patterson wrote *Along Came a Spider* (1992), the first of his Alex Cross murder mysteries. Small wonder that this advertising whiz kid went on to claim the record for the most #1 *New York Times* best sellers (39 of them, so far).

MOONLIGHTING

Some authors are so free-ranging in their interests, no new publication is surprising. But others are so closely identified with a single series or genre that it's virtually impossible to conceive of their doing anything else. Here are some notable side projects or different paths that famous authors have gone down.

H. A. Rey: Forever identified with *Curious George* and *The Man With the Yellow Hat,* Rey was also a keen astronomer in his private life. Frustrated by the quality of existing star guides, he wrote *The Stars: A New Way to See Them* (1952), which remains one of the most popular and easy-to-use books in the field.

Dan Brown: The *Da Vinci Code* author has built an empire out of a fascination with secret codes and ancient mysteries. But it's hard to imagine any cryptographer finding the keys to success in his early musical efforts, which included a self-produced children's cassette *SynthAnimals,* and a self-titled pop music album featuring gems like "976-Love." Sample lyric: "I take you to bed / I push the phone to my head / You make me feel like a man." Yikes.

Haruki Murakami: This award-winning Japanese writer has produced a string of challenging postmodern novels, including 1995's *The Wind-Up Bird Chronicle*—but they're nothing compared with the challenges he faces as a marathon runner and triathlete, a pursuit he chronicled in *What I Talk About When I Talk About Running.* Murakami even competed in a 100-kilometer ultramarathon in 1996.

On the Mound: It's no secret that Beat Generation auteur Jack Kerouac was a talented athlete in high school and during his brief time in college—but until 2009, virtually nobody knew that he also spent most of his life developing and playing a spectacularly complex fantasy baseball game. Chronicled in Isaac Gerwirtz's slim book *Kerouac at Bat: Fantasy Sports and the King of the Beats,* Kerouac's imaginary baseball league featured teams like the Boston Fords and Cincinnati Grays, and players with such colorful names as "Wino Love." Most of Kerouac's work on the game was concentrated in his teenage years, but he wrote imaginary press reports into his 30s and continued to fine-tune the game's formulas for another decade or so beyond that.

HAPPY FAMILIES ARE
ALL ALIKE...

The old adage "Write what you know" never sparks as much controversy as when the writer's eye turns back on his or her own family.

AMIS & AMIS

Kingsley Amis and his son Martin made their names with superficially similar comic novels, set in or around the British university system—Kingsley's *Lucky Jim* (1954) and Martin's *The Rachel Papers* (1973). Though father and son remained close, their opinions of what made for good writing couldn't have diverged more: Kingsley recoiled from Martin's complicated postmodern style, allegedly throwing *Money* (widely viewed as his son's best work) across the room when a character named "Martin Amis" showed up. Likewise, Martin viewed his father's traditional narrative style as a relic: "He was always saying, 'I think you need more sentences like "He put down his drink, got up and left the room,"' and I thought you needed rather fewer of them."

Yet father and son were notorious, apart and together, for their various vices and scandals: Kingsley acknowledged that he was widely viewed as "one of the great drinkers, if not one of the great drunks, of our time," and both were legendary for their love of women—whether they were married to them or not. One of Kingsley's wives took revenge in 1962, scrawling "1 Fat Englishman I F**k Anything" on his back in lipstick as he slept on a Yugoslavian beach, and capturing the moment in a photograph.

MAN OF MANY VICES

Kingsley Amis is remembered as many things, but "model parent" isn't one of them: He allowed his boys, Martin and Philip (the latter named for writer Philip Larkin, a close friend), to smoke one cigarette each on Christmas—starting at age 5. At age 9, he upped the ante to one pack apiece.

BETTER HALF

In the early 1970's, Stephen King's wife, Tabitha, saved him from what could have been the most *horrifying* mistake of his life. King had achieved some meager success, publishing a number of short stories (most of them in men's magazines) and toiling on several novels while he taught at a Maine high school. Discouraged by constant rejection, he tossed the first few pages of another new novel into the trash—but Tabitha fished them out and encouraged him to continue the tale. The book? *Carrie* (1973), which sold more than 1 million copies in paperback and enabled King to devote himself full-time to writing.

THE ICEMAN COMETH

The dark clouds hovering above the works of misanthropic dramatist Eugene O'Neill plagued his family in real life, as well. O'Neill himself was a clinically depressed alcoholic; his mostly estranged sons, Eugene Jr. and Shane, both suffered from addictions of their own and ultimately each took his own life. Daughter Oona seemed to be the one exception to the rule: Her beauty was great enough to elicit daily letters from a smitten J. D. Salinger and a marriage to Charlie Chaplin. But O'Neill disowned Oona over her relationship with Chaplin (who was 36 years her senior).

THE BROTHERS SIMON

Two of Neil Simon's most enduring and recognizable creations, Felix Unger and Oscar Madison of *The Odd Couple,* are partly based on Simon's older brother Danny—himself a radio and TV comedy writer—and Hollywood agent Roy Gerber. The two men shared a home as both went through painful divorces, and their collective foibles inspired Danny, not Neil, to start writing a play about two mismatched male roommates. But Danny couldn't get past page 15 of the script and eventually turned it over to Neil, who awarded his brother one-sixth of the royalties from the hit play in perpetuity. Even though he lived the part, Danny always found it hard to connect with the play: When Neil brought an all-female *Odd Couple* to Broadway in 1985, Danny was brought on to direct . . . but was fired during the tryout tour.

....

> *"Everything, unequivocally, that I learned about comedy writing I learned from Danny Simon. Also, he was very nice."*
>
> —**WOODY ALLEN**

....

THE BITCHES ARE BACK

Novelist Jackie Collins and her actress big sister, Joan Collins—otherwise known as *Dynasty's* Alexis Carrington—have both built thriving careers from creating and portraying the rich, beautiful, and deviously decadent. And each has at least dipped a toe into the other's waters: Jackie started out as an actress in the 1950s and '60s, before turning full-time to writing books like *The Stud*

(1960) and its sequel, *The Bitch* (1979), both of which became films starring her older sister. Joan has been known to put pen to paper, too: In addition to the requisite beauty and lifestyle books, she has written six best-selling novels of her own (starting with 1988's *Prime Time*).

HARD TO BELIEVE

Though she's known for creating scheming, beautiful, fashion-obsessed female characters, Jackie Collins claims to have never had a facial or a professional manicure—but admits to being a "makeup-aholic."

BIG BROTHER, CIRCA 1940

Had network television been in business in 1940, it might have produced an early installment of the reality show *Big Brother* by training its cameras on the fascinating artistic and social experiment known as February House. Dreamed up (literally) by headstrong, idiosyncratic George Davis, the fiction editor of *Harper's Bazaar,* February House was an experiment in communal living by some of the most notable names of the time, many of whom pooled their funds to live in a huge four-story walkup in Brooklyn Heights. This ad hoc family included:

W. H. Auden: Davis enticed him with a promise of low rent and a view of the Brooklyn Bridge; Auden brought British composer Benjamin Britten (and his partner, Peter Pears) with him and wrote the libretto for Britten's *Paul Bunyan* while living there. For a time, the mostly straight-laced Auden acted like the father of the group, setting rules for everything from chores to dining-table conversation—but was also tormented by his unfaithful 20-year-old male lover and ultimately was driven away by the increasingly rowdy antics of later arrivals.

Carson McCullers: One of the original tenants, McCullers moved in, partially to expand her circle of friends outside of her troubled marriage. She became known in the house for cooking her signature dish "Spuds Carson," made from potatoes and any other leftover food she could find. Her creativity at February House wasn't limited to the kitchen—it was there that she laid the groundwork for *The Member of the Wedding* and *The Ballad of the Sad Café*.

Gypsy Rose Lee: The legendary stripper took up residence in part to burnish her serious-artist credentials, picking Davis's brain for assistance in finishing *The G-String Murders,* a mystery novel starring herself as the sleuth uncovering a series of strip-club killings.

Jane and Paul Bowles: The promiscuously bisexual couple brought a new element of wildness to February House, roping in temporary guests like Salvador Dali and his wife, Gala, and sparking feuds with other residents. Paul and Britten quarreled over where each would place his piano, with Auden siding with Britten, forever damaging his friendship with Bowles. The Bowleses famously chased each other around their bedroom one night, with Jane screaming "I'll get you for this; you've ruined my uterus!" Yet during their stay, Jane began *Two Sophisticated Ladies* and Paul shifted his focus from music to fiction.

ALL IN THE FAMILY

The grandfather of civil disobedience, advocate Henry David Thoreau led the first recorded student protest in the United States ... against the quality of food at Harvard University. His group's slogan? "Behold, our Butter stinketh!"

GOSSIP: GIRLS

Philosophers Jean-Paul Sartre and Simone de Beauvoir (intriguingly nicknamed *le Castor*, or "the Beaver," by an early boyfriend) were in their 20s when they first met in Paris in 1929; and against all odds, the beautiful Beauvoir and short, half-blind Sartre formed a lifelong relationship as unconventional as their philosophies. Though the two were physical with each other at the start of their "romance," their love affair later consisted primarily of sharing stories of sexual exploits with other people— or even assisting each other in the seduction of young women. On one occasion, when one of these girls fell into an affair with Beauvoir but refused Sartre's advances, he duly moved on to the girl's sister ... and when the seduction was finally consummated, he ran to Beauvoir to share the details.

"The word love has by no means the same sense for both sexes, and this is one cause of the serious misunderstandings that divide them."

—SIMONE DE BEAUVOIR

FANTASTIC FRIENDS

It was probably inevitable that C. S. Lewis and J. R. R. Tolkien would become friends (and at times, rivals): Both were World War I veterans, scholars of medieval and early modern literature, and lovers of ancient Icelandic myths. At Oxford University Tolkien welcomed Lewis into a group called the Coalbiters, a *Dead Poets Society*–type club for men who enjoyed sitting around reading old Icelandic tales (in the original Norse, naturally) with each other. Tolkien was also instrumental in Lewis's conversion to Christianity—without which Lewis would probably never have written the *Chronicles of Narnia*. Lewis praised "the inexhaustible fertility" of Tolkien's imagination, while Tolkien spoke of the "unpayable debt" he owed Lewis for his support and encouragement.

But like many longtime friends, the two could be catty: Tolkien disapproved of the overt Christian symbolism of the *Narnia* books, calling them "about as bad as can be." Lewis struck back by creating John Ransom, the hero of his "Space Trilogy," as a not-entirely-flattering version of Tolkien; Tolkien put some of Lewis's mannerisms into the character Treebeard, the loquacious but slow-talking leader of the *Lord of the Rings'* Ents. But the two could always rally together in their dislike of Modernist literature, as in Lewis's poetic takedown of T. S. Eliot:

> *For twenty years I've stared my level best*
> *To see if evening—any evening—would suggest*
> *A patient etherised upon a table;*
> *In vain. I simply wasn't able.*

UNTIMELY DEMISES

Far too many talented writers have ended their own lives. In memoriam, a look at a few:

- The poet Hart Crane (1899–1932) was just 33 years old when he died in 1932. The author of the epic poem "The Bridge" (1930), Crane had made little progress on newer works in later years as his drinking problem escalated. On a ship returning to New York from Mexico, Crane was involved in a fight in the sailors' quarters, then threw himself into the Gulf of Mexico.

- *Mrs. Dalloway* author Virginia Woolf (1882–1941) and her husband, author and critic Leonard Woolf, had made preparations to commit suicide together in the event of a Nazi invasion of Britain. But Virginia, a longtime sufferer of depression, instead drowned herself alone in a river near the Woolf's country house. The note she left for her husband read, in part, "I have a feeling I shall go mad. I cannot go on longer in these terrible times. I hear voices and cannot concentrate on my work. I have fought against it but cannot fight any longer."

- Always a heavy drinker but especially so in later years, Ernest Hemingway (1899–1961) was given electroconvulsive therapy to treat depression. Some critics theorized that he was so disturbed by the resulting memory loss that he shot himself with his favorite shotgun. Obituaries at the time noted his wife's statement that the gun had accidentally gone off while Hemingway was cleaning it, but "Papa" was a known firearms expert, unlikely to make such a novice mistake. Hemingway's father had also committed suicide.

- The first poet to posthumously win a Pulitzer prize, Sylvia Plath (1932–63) left a note for a neighbor to call a doctor, sealed off the rooms between her kitchen and her children with wet cloths, and turned on the oven. Several years later, the longtime mistress of Plath's husband, Ted Hughes (a renowned poet), killed herself in a similar fashion, with even more-tragic results: The couple's 4-year-old daughter died as well.

- John Kennedy Toole (1933–69) ran away from home following a fight with his mother in January 1969. He was found asphyxiated in his car several months later, after a road trip that took him to the Georgia home of fellow Southern writer Flannery O'Connor. *A Confederacy of Dunces* lay in Toole's desk drawer for more than a decade after his death, until his mother finally persuaded Walker Percy to read it.

- The exact date of *Trout Fishing in America* (1967) author Richard Brautigan's (1935–84) death has never been determined; he had clearly been dead from a self-inflicted gunshot wound for several weeks when his body was found. Strangely, it was only after his death that Brautigan's father found out about the existence of a famous son: Brautigan's mother and father had separated before he was born.

- Perhaps fittingly for a man who, as a young writer, investigated why Ernest Hemingway had committed suicide (and made off with the elk horns that hung over the entrance to Hemingway's Idaho home), Hunter S. Thompson (1937–2005) shot himself in February 2005. He left a note, entitled "Football Season Is Over" that read:

> *"No More Games. No More Bombs. No More Walking. No More Fun. No More Swimming. 67.*

*That is 17 years past 50. 17 more than I needed
or wanted. Boring. I am always bitchy. No Fun—
for anybody. 67. You are getting Greedy. Act your
old age. Relax—This won't hurt."*

- After suffering depression for most of his adult life, David Foster Wallace (1962–2008) hanged himself in September 2008. He had stopped taking Nardil, an antidepressant, more than a year before his death. Wallace had taken extreme measures—including electroconvulsive therapy—trying to alleviate his mental illness.

BEDTIME FOR GONZO

Hunter S. Thompson's 2005 memorial celebration was as irreverent as Thompson himself. According to Thompson's wishes, a 15-story cannon modeled on Thompson's "gonzo fist" (a double-thumbed fist clutching a peyote button, a symbol first used in his 1970 campaign for sheriff of Aspen), shot fireworks filled with Thompson's ashes into the air. The actor Johnny Depp, who portrayed Thompson in a movie version of *Fear and Loathing in Las Vegas* (1998), covered most of the cost of construction. As the fireworks erupted and ashes fell on some 250 guests in attendance, actor Harry Dean Stanton said, "I have never seen an event like this. And I'm old. Very old."

DEATH BY MISADVENTURE

These writers were legends in their own times, but their lives didn't have the most glorious of endings.

Li Po (701–762): The Chinese poet is said to have drowned after falling out of a boat, trying to embrace the moon's reflection in the water.

Christopher Marlowe (1564–93): The infamously hot-tempered playwright (who also is believed to have served as a spy for Queen Elizabeth I) was stabbed in the head, allegedly over payment of a bar tab—though some believe it was a politically motivated murder.

Edgar Allan Poe (1809–49): For almost 150 years, Poe's death was believed to have resulted from complications of alcoholism: He was found unconscious outside a Baltimore saloon and died four days later, after slipping in and out of a coma. But in 1996 Dr. R. Michael Benitez reviewed Poe's case and concluded that the writer had more likely died from rabies, possibly contracted from one of his own pets.

Leo Tolstoy (1828–1910): At age 82, the renowned author of *War and Peace* left his estate in the hands of his secretary, Vladimir Chertkov, and embarked on a new life as a wandering ascetic—but soon after died of pneumonia at a remote railway station.

Sherwood Anderson (1876–1941): After accidentally swallowing part of a toothpick embedded in an hors d'oeuvre at a cocktail party, Anderson contracted peritonitis and died a few days later.

Tennessee Williams (1911–83): Under the influence of drugs and alcohol in a New York hotel room, the playwright choked to death on the cap from a bottle of eyedrops.

....

"Life does not cease to be funny when people die any more than it ceases to be serious when people laugh."

—GEORGE BERNARD SHAW

....

INDEX

ABOUT THE AUTHORS

C. Alan Joyce is the editor-in-chief of the #1 best-selling *The World Almanac and Book of Facts*. Joyce was previously a freelance writer and editor, with years of experience in reference publishing—and a lifelong addiction to reference books of all kinds. He is the former executive editor of *The New York Times Almanac* and *The New York Times Guide to Essential Knowledge*.

Sarah Janssen is an editor of *The World Almanac and Book of Facts* and other diverse titles, focusing primarily on arts and media, consumer information, history, and sports. She currently lives in Brooklyn, NY.

Enjoy These Other Reader's Digest Bestsellers

Featuring all the memory-jogging tips you'll ever need to know, this fun little book will help you recall hundreds of important facts using simple, easy-to-remember mnemonics from your school days.

$14.95 hardcover
ISBN 978-0-7621-0917-3

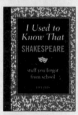

Make learning fun again with these light-hearted pages that are packed with important theories, phrases, and those long-forgotten "rules" you once learned in school.

$14.95 hardcover
ISBN 978-0-7621-0995-1

Capturing the unbelievable scope of Shakespeare's influence, this book will surprise and delight you not only with fascinating facts and little-known details of his life but also with the surprising legacy of the language and phrases inherited from his works.

$14.95 hardcover
ISBN 978-1-60652-246-2

Confused about when to use "its" or "it's" or the correct spelling of "principal" or "principle"? Avoid language pitfalls and let this entertaining and practical guide improve both your speaking and writing skills.

$14.95 hardcover
ISBN 978-1-60652-026-0

Do you know who really designed and sewed the first flag? It wasn't Betsy Ross! The answer to this and hundreds of other fascinating myth-debunking facts of U.S. history will delight history buffs and trivia lovers alike.

$14.95 hardcover
ISBN 978-1-60652-035-2